Creative Bible Activities for Children Series

Life and Lessons of Jesus — Vol. 2

Jesus' Ministry

Copyright © 1991 by Tracy Leffingwell Harrast.
Published by Cook Communications Ministries.

Printed in the United States of America.

All puzzles and Bible activities are based on the NIV.

Scripture taken from the Holy Bible, New International Version,
Copyright ©1973, 1978, 1984 International Bible Society.
Used by permission of Zondervan Publishing House.

Cover Illustration by Gary Locke

Cover Design by Todd Mock and Mike Riester

Interior Illustrations by Anne Kennedy

Interior Design by Tabb Associates, Mike Riester, and Cheryl Morton

ISBN #0781438489   101842

Life and Lessons of Jesus Vol. 2—Jesus Works Miracles

CONTENTS

Jesus Works Miracles

Jesus Heals

Jesus Teaches Me to Pray

Jesus Works Miracles

Palestine, Where Jesus Served

Draw a line from each miracle to the place where Jesus worked it.

1. Jesus changes water to wine at a wedding in Cana.

2. Jesus fills a net with fish at the Sea of Galilee.

3. Jesus calms a storm on the Sea of Galilee.

4. Jesus feeds thousands at Bethsaida.

5. Jesus feeds thousands at a mountain near the Sea of Galilee.

6. Jesus walks on the Sea of Galilee.

7. While in Capernaum, Jesus sends Peter to find a coin in a fish's mouth.

8. Jesus makes a fig tree wither in Bethany.

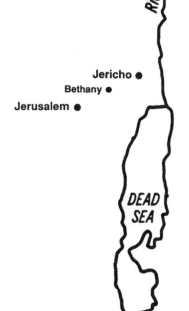

MEDITERRANEAN SEA

N

Capernaum   Bethsaida

SEA of GALILEE

Cana

River Jordan

Jericho

Bethany

Jerusalem

DEAD SEA

DESERT

Miracles Are A-maze-ing

Answer these questions and then see if your answers are right by using them to direct you through the maze. If they're correct, you'll go from the beginning to the end without getting stuck.

1. Are miracles real?

2. Is a miracle a trick?

3. Are miracles supposed to entertain?

4. Do miracles help people's faith in God become stronger?

5. Is it possible for miracles to happen today?

6. Are miracles done with magic?

7. Is the greatest miracle that Jesus rose from the dead so we can live forever with God?

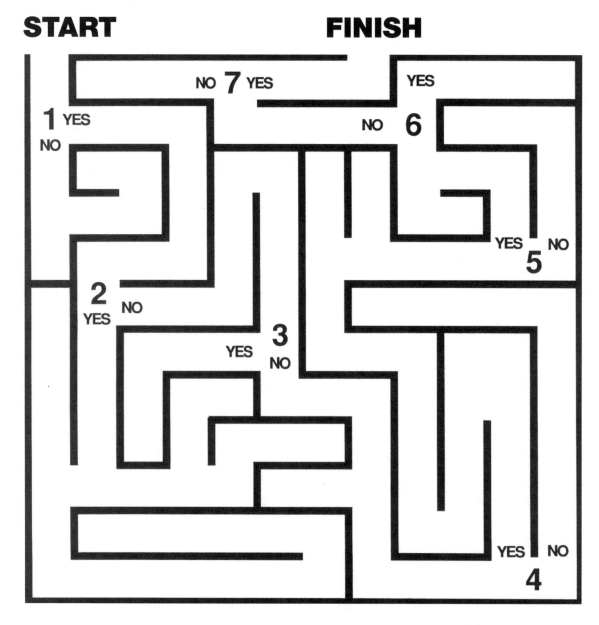

Miracle Matchup

Put the letter of each miracle under the picture it matches.

A. Jesus turns water to wine   D. Jesus feeds thousands from five loaves and two fish

B. Jesus fills a net with fish   E. Jesus walks on the sea

C. Jesus calms a storm   F. Jesus knows a coin will be in a fish's mouth

Jesus Changes Water to Wine

When you come to a scrambled word in the story, unscramble it and write in the correct word. This way you can read about Jesus' first miracle.

One day Jesus, His disciples (followers), and his **hmtore** _____ (Mary) attended a **wgednid** _____.
After a while, the host ran out of **inwe** _____, and Mary told Jesus. Jesus **kesda** _____ what Mary wanted Him to do. Mary didn't **sawnre** _____, but she told the servants to do whatever Jesus told **meth** _____ to do.

There were six **eotns** _____ water pots there, which could hold **wnttye** _____ or thirty gallons each. Jesus said to **lilf** _____ the pots with **rawet** _____, and the servants did. Jesus then told one of the servants to give **eosm** _____ to the host of the wedding **sefat** _____.

The wedding host didn't believe the wine he tasted had once been water. He said he was happily surprised that the groom had **vased** _____ the best wine for last.

Jesus did this first **rimcale** _____ in Cana of Galilee and His disciples believed that He was God's Son.

☐ *Draw a star in this box when you've read the story in John 2:1-11.*

Jesus' First Miracle

Jesus   Disciples   Mary

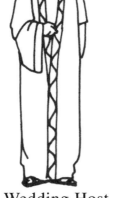

Wedding Host   Servant   Servant

Color these characters from the first miracle Jesus worked. Then cut out the figures, and tape them to spoons to make puppets.

Put on a puppet show for your family and friends in which puppets perform the story of Jesus changing the water into wine. For a special effect, you might want to pour a grape drink mix into water to show the water changing into wine. Be sure to point out that Jesus used power instead of powder!

Note: When you're finished playing with your puppets, remove the tape from them, place them in an envelope, and tape the envelope inside this book so you will have them to play with again and again.

Jesus Fills the Net

Using the code, put a letter in each blank to finish the story.
When you're done, enjoy reading the story.

CODE				
A=26	G=20	M=14	S=8	Y=2
B=25	H=19	N=13	T=7	Z=1
C=24	I=18	O=12	U=6	
D=23	J=17	P=11	V=5	
E=22	K=16	Q=10	W=4	
F=21	L=15	R=9	X=3	

One day _ _ _ _ _ (17 22 8 6 8) told _ _ _ _ _ (8 18 14 12 13) _ _ _ _ _ _ (11 22 7 22 9) to take his _ _ _ _ (25 12 26 7) into deep _ _ _ _ _ (4 26 7 22 9) and let _ _ _ _ (23 12 4 13) his _ _ _ (13 22 7) to _ _ _ _ _ (24 26 7 24 19) a lot of _ _ _ _ (21 18 8 19). _ _ _ _ _ (8 18 14 12 13) _ _ _ _ _ (11 22 7 22 9) said, "We _ _ _ _ _ _ (21 18 8 19 22 23) all _ _ _ _ _ (13 18 20 19 7) and didn't _ _ _ _ _ (24 26 7 24 19) anything, but I'll let _ _ _ _ (23 12 4 13) the _ _ _ (13 22 7) again anyway." After he _ _ _ _ _ _ _ (23 9 12 11 11 22 23) it, the _ _ _ (13 22 7) filled up with so many _ _ _ _ (21 18 8 19) that it _ _ _ _ _ (25 9 12 16 22). The _ _ _ _ (21 18 8 19) filled two _ _ _ _ _ (8 19 18 11 8) and the boats began to _ _ _ _ (8 18 13 16).

_ _ _ _ _ (8 18 14 12 13) _ _ _ _ _ (11 22 7 22 9) and everyone else were _ _ _ _ _ _ (26 14 26 1 22 23). Simon Peter _ _ _ _ (21 22 15 15) at Jesus' _ _ _ _ (16 13 22 22 8). Jesus said, "From now on, you will _ _ _ _ _ (24 26 7 24 19) men." He meant that Simon Peter and his fishing _ _ _ _ _ _ _ (11 26 9 7 13 22 9 8) would _ _ _ _ _ (25 9 18 13 20) _ _ _ _ _ _ (11 22 12 11 15 22) into the _ _ _ _ _ _ (16 18 13 20 23 12 14) of _ _ _ (20 12 23).

☐ *Draw a star in this box when you've read the story in Luke 5:3-11.*

Become a "Fisher of Men"

Jesus wants us to be fishers of men like His disciples. He wants us to tell others about Him so they will want to follow Him, too. Sometimes it's hard to think of ways to tell people about Jesus. Here are a few "hooks" you can use to get your friends interested in talking about Jesus. *As you talk to your friends about Jesus, write their names on the fish.*

Ask your friend if you can tell him or her a story about a miracle Jesus did.

"I read an amazing story today."

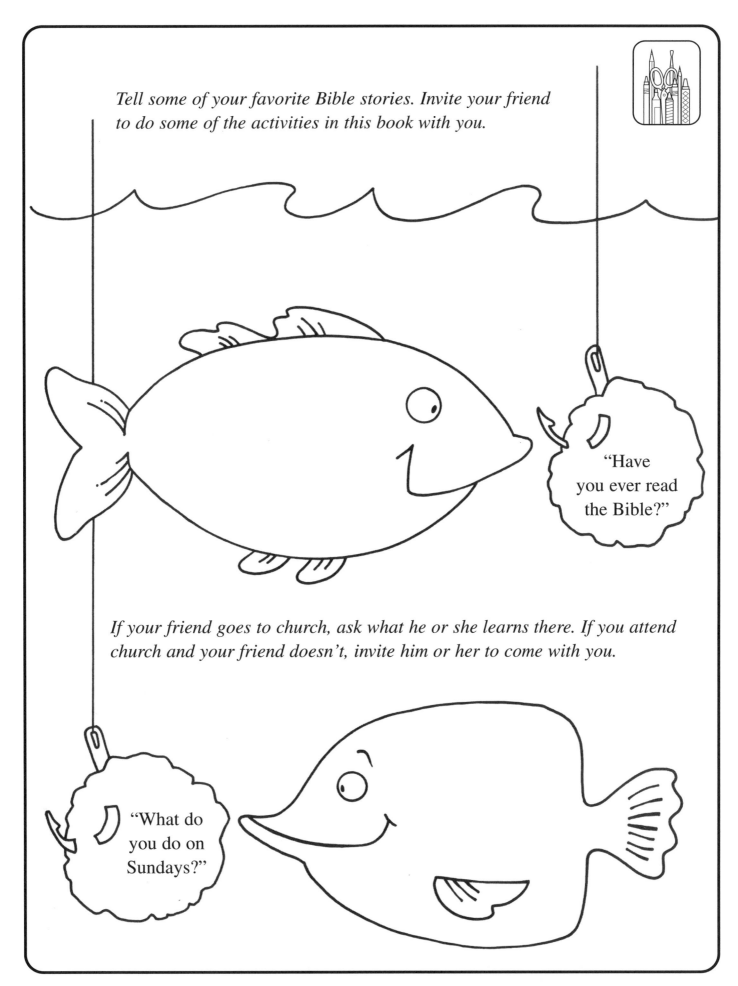

Tell some of your favorite Bible stories. Invite your friend to do some of the activities in this book with you.

"Have you ever read the Bible?"

If your friend goes to church, ask what he or she learns there. If you attend church and your friend doesn't, invite him or her to come with you.

"What do you do on Sundays?"

Make a Sponge Fish

Make this fun bath toy for yourself or your younger brothers or sisters to remind you of the miracle of the fish in the nets.

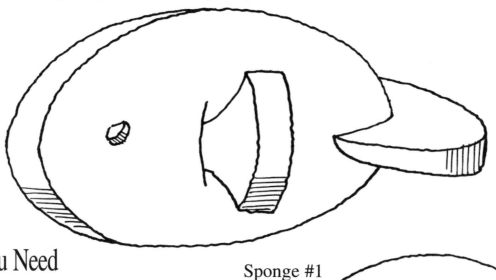

What You Need

- two oval sponges that are different colors

- pencil

- scissors

- a little help from a grown-up

Sponge #1

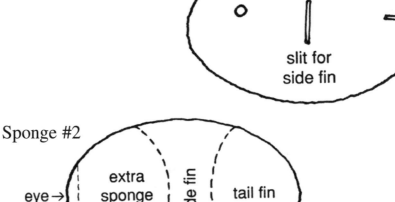

slit for tail fin

slit for side fin

Sponge #2

eye →   extra sponge   side fin   tail fin

What You Do

1. *Use the pencil to poke a hole for the eye in sponge #1. Use the scissors to cut slits in sponge #1 for the two fins.*

2. *Cut sponge #2 into four pieces shaped like these.*

3. *Poke the eyepiece cut from sponge #2 into the eyehole on sponge #1. Poke the side fin cut from sponge #2 into the side fin slit on sponge #1. And poke the tail fin cut from sponge #2 through the tail fin slit on sponge #1.*

Make a Boat

One day Jesus and His disciples wanted to cross the Sea of Galilee. You can read what happened when Jesus and His disciples crossed the Sea of Galilee in Matthew 8:22-27; Mark 4:35-41; and Luke 8:22-25.

Make this "boat," and pretend your bathtub or a puddle is the Sea of Galilee. When you've read the story, act it out with your boat.

What You Need

- cardboard milk carton
- stapler
- scissors
- piece of clay
- drinking straw
- paper hole punch
- square piece of paper

What You Do

1. *Staple the top of the milk carton shut. Then cut out one side of the carton.*

2. *To make the sail, punch two holes on opposite sides of the square of paper. You'll want the holes punched in the center and not too close to the edge. Next, poke the straw through the holes for your sail.*

3. *Place a wad of clay inside the carton, near the stapled top, and stick the straw into the clay so it stands up straight.*

4. *Go float your boat!*

Draw a star in this box when you've read the story in Matthew 8:23-27; Mark 4:35-41; and Luke 8:22-25.

Caught in a Storm

The disciples were terrified that they would drown at sea. They woke Jesus and asked Him to save them. Jesus stood up and told the winds and the sea to be calm and still. Immediately, the wind stopped and the sea became calm. *Color this picture.*

Have you ever been caught in a bad storm or another scary situation?
Write about how you felt.

_____

_____

_____

_____

_____

_____

How would you have felt if you were in the boat with Jesus and the disciples when that storm came up? *Write what you would have done.*

_____

_____

_____

_____

_____

_____

How would you have felt if you saw Jesus calm the storm? *Write what this miracle shows you about Jesus.*

_____

_____

_____

_____

_____

_____

Tossed About in the Storm

While Jesus was sound asleep in the rear part of the ship, a terrible storm arose. The waves crashed over the ship and filled part of it. *Find the ship and ten other items in this storm. Look for a ship, an anchor, a treasure chest, a fish, a sea gull, a fishing pole, a net, a shell, a sandal, a pillow, and a candle.*

See the Sea

Make a sea in a bottle. To show what the sea looked like during the storm while Jesus was asleep, shake the jar. Keep it still to show what happened when Jesus said, "Peace, be still."

What You Need

- small, clean jar with lid
- white vinegar
- blue and green food coloring
- salad oil
- salt

What You Do

1. *Fill the jar half full with white vinegar.*

2. *Add one or two drops of food coloring.*

3. *Screw on the lid and shake the jar until the food coloring and vinegar are mixed together.*

4. *Open the jar and add salad oil until the jar is full. Because sea water is salty, you might want to add a teaspoon of salt, too. Close the jar tightly and you have a sea in a bottle.*

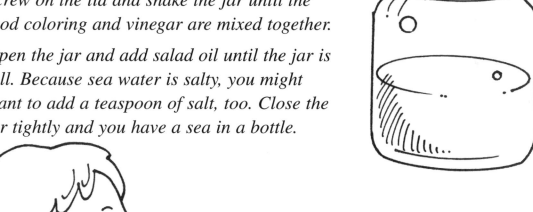

The Missing Word

The apostles were missing it. Sometimes we don't have it either when we're afraid. But trusting in Jesus makes this stronger. *To find the hidden word, fill in each space with a letter with the color it matches. If a space doesn't have a letter, don't color it.*

G=Green   R=Red   Y=Yellow   P=Purple   O=Orange   B=Blue

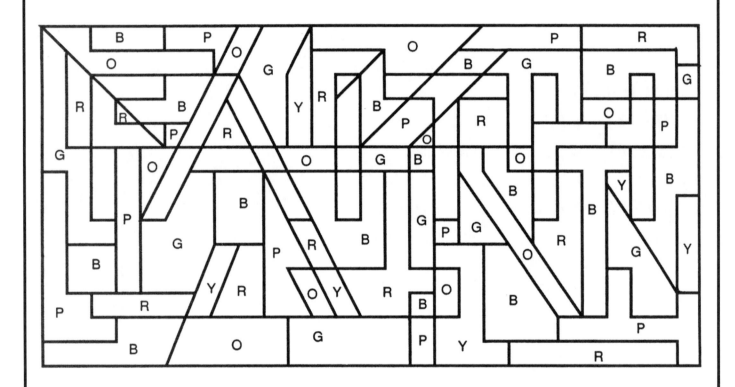

Write the word from the puzzle in the blanks below.

Jesus asked the disciples why they were afraid and why they didn't have more _____. Our _____ grows when we trust the Lord to answer our prayers and ask Him to help us. Then we aren't afraid.

A Puzzling Story

Fit each of the underlined words from the story into the puzzle.

One evening Jesus and His disciples needed to cross the **SEA** of Galilee. A terrible storm **AROSE**, and the **DISCIPLES** were **AFRAID**. They woke up Jesus and asked Him to help them. He performed a **MIRACLE**. If we have **FAITH**, the Lord will perform miracles in our lives, too.

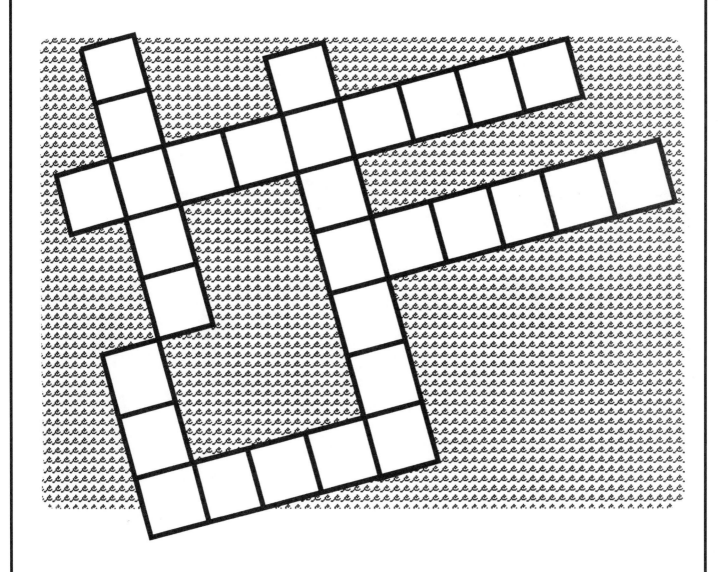

Rely on God

The disciples were amazed when Jesus calmed the storm. They wondered what kind of man would be obeyed by the wind and sea. Jesus had the power to calm the winds and the sea, and He helped His disciples when they were afraid. He can help you, too. *Write down a problem you have or draw a picture, and then write a prayer, asking the Lord to help you with it.*

MY PROBLEM

MY PRAYER FOR THE LORD'S HELP

Jesus Feeds Thousands of People

Finish the story by putting these words in the correct blanks. Use each only once:
thanks, desert, loaves, boy, fish, leave, faint, groups, twelve, heaven

One evening after Jesus taught a crowd in the _____, His disciples asked Him to send the people away so they could buy themselves food in the village. Jesus said, "They don't need to _____. You give them something to eat." Andrew said, "There's a young _____ here with five loaves of bread and two small _____, but that's not enough to feed this crowd of people." Jesus said, "Bring the boy to me." Jesus also asked the people to sit on the grass in _____ of fifties and hundreds. Then Jesus held the five loaves and two fish, looked up to _____, and gave thanks. He gave the bread and fish to the disciples, and they passed out the food to the people. More than 5,000 people were fed that day. Afterward, the disciples picked up _____ baskets of leftovers.

Another time, Jesus had been teaching more than 4,000 people for three days in the wilderness. Now Jesus knew that they were hungry and didn't want to send them away without eating because they might _____. The disciples only had seven _____ of bread and a few fish. Jesus gave _____, divided the bread and fish, and gave them to the disciples, who in turn gave the food to the people. Once again, everyone in the crowd was fed, and this time, there were seven baskets of leftovers.

☐ *Draw a star in this box when you've read the stories in Matthew 14:15-21; Mark 6:33-44; Luke 9:11-17; John 6:5-15; Matthew 15:32-38; and Mark 8:1-9.*

My 'Loaves and Fish'

Just as God took care of the people's needs, God blesses us every day with food and many other things we need, even though He doesn't usually do it in such an amazing way as in the story you just read. *Write or draw some of the things you're thankful for on the loaves and fish. Remember to thank God for your "loaves and fish" when you pray.*

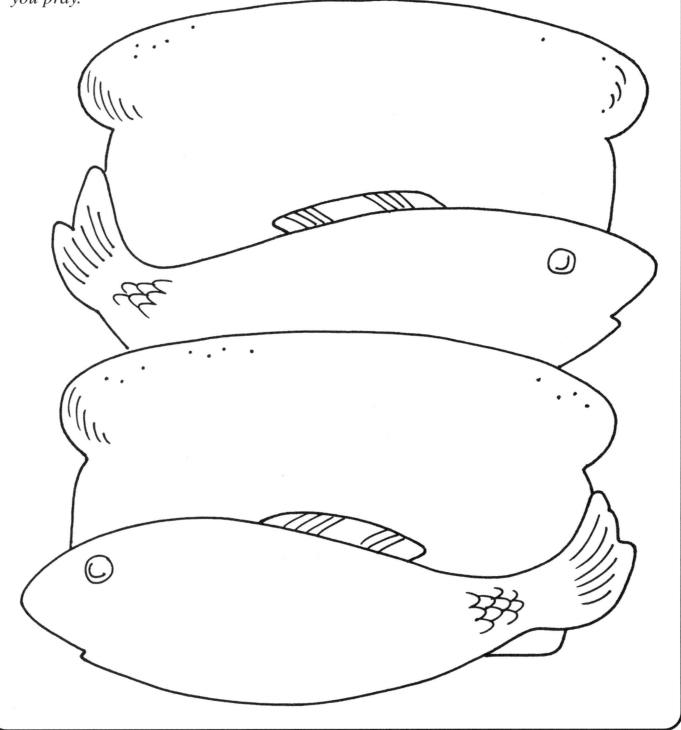

Make a Diorama

Read the story on page 24 again, and then make a diorama (a scene in a box) of Jesus feeding the crowds. With a little imagination and some things from around the house you can recreate the setting of this miracle. The following list of materials and directions are only suggestions to get you thinking.

What You Need

- box
- scissors
- colored paper, self-adhesive paper, or fabric
- glue

- tissue paper
- tape
- pencil
- drawing or construction paper
- paints

- crayons
- dirt, pebbles, or moss
- modeling clay
- foil
- slice of bread

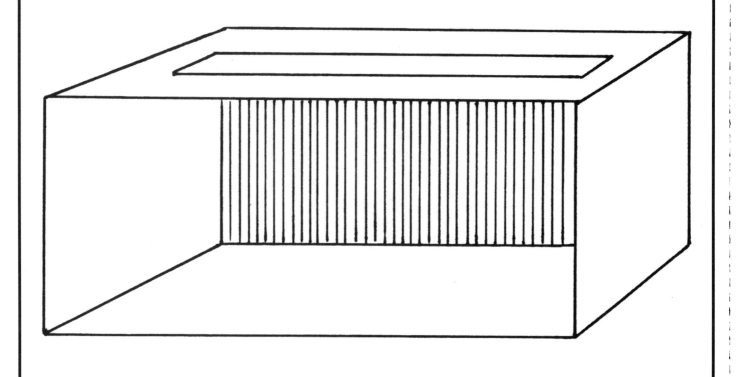

What You Do

1. Cut a rectangular hole on one side of the box. This will be the top of your diorama, and will let in light.

2. Glue colored paper, self-adhesive paper, or fabric to the box, leaving the light hole uncovered. To cover the light hole, tape tissue paper on the inside of the box.

3. Trace the bottom of the box onto a piece of drawing or construction paper. This will make a background for your diorama. Cut out the rectangle, and then paint the scene, draw it, or glue on paper cutouts. Include sky, mountains, people sitting on the grass. Use your imagination and creativity. When you're done with the background, glue it to the back of the diorama.

4. Start making the foreground scene. First, glue dirt, pebbles, moss, or shredded green tissue to the bottom of the diorama.

5. Make figures of Jesus, the disciples, and even the little boy from clay. You could also add fun details like real rocks for the disciples to sit on, baskets, fish made by wadding up tiny pieces of foil, and small pieces of a slice of bread shaped to look like loaves.

Jesus Walks on Water

One day after He finished teaching, Jesus went to the mountains to pray. Meanwhile, His disciples decided to board a ship and cross the sea. While the disciples were at sea, a strong wind blew in and the waves began tossing the ship around.

When Jesus finished praying, it was early morning. Suddenly the disciples saw a figure walking on the water. They were afraid, convinced it was a ghost. Then the figure called out. "Don't be afraid. It's Me, Jesus!"

"Lord," Peter answered, "Lord, if it's really You, ask me to come to You on the water."

Jesus said, "Come."

Peter got out of the ship and, to his amazement, he began to walk on the water toward Jesus. But when Peter noticed how strong the wind was, he was afraid and began to sink. "Lord, save me," Peter shouted. Jesus reached out and caught Peter.

"You don't have much faith. Why did you doubt Me?" Jesus asked. When they entered the ship, the wind stopped. All the other disciples were amazed and worshiped Jesus. "It's true—You are the Son of God," they said.

After reading this story, number the pictures in the order they belong. The first one is done for you.

JESUS WALKING ON WATER

A

JESUS ON SHIP WITH OTHERS WORSHIPPING HIM

B

JESUS PRAYING ON THE MOUNTAINTOP

C **1**

JESUS REACHING TO A SINKING PETER

D

PETER WALKING ON WATER

E

BOAT ON A STORMY SEA

F

Draw a star in this box when you've read the stories in Matthew 14:22, 23; Mark 6:45-52; and John 6:17-21.

Would Your Faith Sink or Float?

In tough situations, would your faith in God's help sink or float? *Read each situation, and then check either yes or no. Answer these questions as honestly as you can. Then use your answers for the activity on the next page.*

You're worried about a big test in math. Would you have enough faith to trust God to help you remember what you studied?

YES   NO

Your sister is really sick. You've been praying for her for days, but she's not getting any better. Would you have enough faith to trust God to take care of your sister, even when you don't see any answers to your prayer right away?

YES   NO

Your parents are worried that your old car is going to stop running. Would you have enough faith to trust God to supply a new car or to keep the old one running a little longer?

YES   NO

One of the kids at school got you in trouble with your teacher when you weren't doing anything wrong. Would you have enough faith to trust God to help you forgive him and make things right between the two of you?

YES   NO

Faith to Float

While Peter was walking on the water toward Jesus, he was afraid and began to sink. Do you think you would have trusted Jesus enough to walk to Him on the water? For fun, try this activity.

What You Need

- two clear drinking glasses
- boiled egg
- waterproof marker
- paper
- pencil
- tape
- water
- salt

What You Do

1. *Answer the questions on page 30.*

2. *Draw a face on a boiled egg with a waterproof marker.*

3. *Fill two clear drinking glasses half full of water. Label one "yes" and the other "no."*

4. *Add three tablespoons of salt to the "yes" glass and stir until the salt dissolves.*

5. *Reread each question and gently drop the egg into the cup labeled the way you answered to see whether you would have shown faith or not. This activity is especially fun to do with friends who don't know there is salt in the water. Ask them the questions and drop the egg in the glass for each answer.*

Make a String Picture

Read about the miracle of the coin in the fish's mouth on page 37. Then make a string picture using the pattern on page 35. You may want an adult to help you.

What You Need

• thin, white, 8 1/2" x 11" piece of cardboard or poster board
• dull needle
• coin or piece of foil
• colored thread or embroidery floss

What You Do

1. Place the fish pattern from page 33 on top of the cardboard.

2. Use a dull needle to punch holes through the dots marked on the pattern.

3. Remove the pattern and glue a coin or circle made of foil to cardboard as shown on the pattern.

4. Sew colored thread or embroidery floss through the holes, following numbers in order on the pattern.

5. When you finish, the cardboard should have threads where there are lines on this pattern.

Make a String Picture

Do not cut this out, punch holes through it onto the cardboard.

The Coin in a Fish's Mouth

1 day some asked &

2 pay a 4 the .

 told  2 2 the &

2  . told 2 O+

the of the 1st he caught

& there   a N+side.

 Jesus   Peter   Temple

Draw a star in this box when you've read the story in Matthew 17:24-27.

Jesus Withers a Fig Tree

Read the story and then find each of the bold words in the puzzle on the next page.

One day **Jesus** was **hungry** and when He saw a **fig tree**, He went to it **hoping** to find **fruit**. There wasn't any, and Jesus said, "Let no fruit **grow** on you from now **on**." The **next** day the tree dried up from its **roots**. The **disciples** (followers of Jesus) marveled and Jesus said to them, "If you have **faith** and do not **doubt**, you will be able to do things like what was **done** to the fig tree, and you will also **say** to this **mountain**, 'Go, throw yourself into the **sea**,' and it will **be** done. If you believe, you will **receive** whatever you **ask** for in **prayer**."

Draw a star in this box when you've read the story in Matthew 21:18-22 and Mark 11:12-14, 20-26.

```
R K J L P N R E Y A R P B Z C R D L
G O M D R K S K M E R I A L K I D P
J R S V B A T H U N G R Y N S P Q V
E P O C D I O M J R K N B C Z L B A
S L J W N B O L Y A S Q I U R F E S
U T P U G H R F R M P Y T P R L K
S S R E M O V E D S L A G S L U I D
P F S F I G S I T E R C T Y U I E E
A W O V L N Y C S X F D O U B T V L
R I R W E C T E W R O V I R O S I L
J V O X Z F A L H O P I N G T D N E
B E T T I S W O T N V R W F R O G V
W X S R Y E V I E C E R S T S N S R
L O T V E S F R H T I A F E B E N A
H E R K V E L M S Z N I A T N U O M
```

Jesus Fills the Nets Again!

After Jesus died on the cross, He came back to life and visited His disciples several times. One time He appeared at the shore. It was morning and Peter and the other disciples had been fishing all night, but hadn't caught a thing.

From the shore, Jesus asked if they had caught anything. His disciples replied no. Jesus then told them to put their net on the right side of the boat. When they did this, they caught so many fish that they couldn't pull in the net. Instead, they had to drag it behind in a smaller boat.

This miracle may have reminded the disciples of when Jesus first called them "fishers of men." It probably helped them remember the other miracles they had seen Jesus do in the past. *Play this game with a friend to see how well you remember the miracles you learned about in this book.*

What You Need

- fish from page 39
- paper clips
- bowl
- string
- stick
- small magnet
- envelope

What You Do

1. *Cut out the fish on page 39 and put a paper clip on each fish. You'll notice that each fish has a miracle written on it. Place each fish face-down in a bowl.*

2. *Make a fishing pole by tying a string to a stick. Use a magnet for "bait" and tie it to the end of the string.*

3. *Take turns catching the fish. For every fish a player catches, that person has to tell the story of that miracle in order to get a point.*

4. *After the last fish has been caught and its story told, add up the points. The player with the most points wins.*

5. *When you're finished, place the fish in an envelope. Then tape the envelope inside this book so you can play the game another time.*

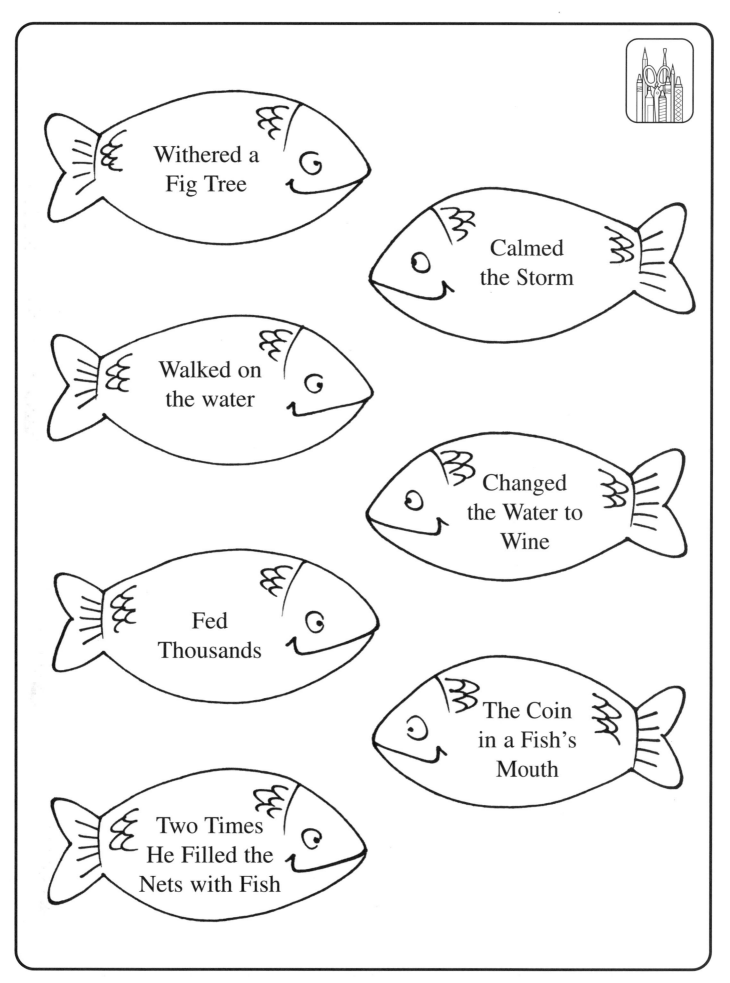

Withered a Fig Tree

Calmed the Storm

Walked on the water

Changed the Water to Wine

Fed Thousands

The Coin in a Fish's Mouth

Two Times He Filled the Nets with Fish

I Did It!

COMPLETED	DATE	COMPLETED	DATE
☐ Palestine, Where Jesus Lived	_____	☐ A Puzzling Story	_____
☐ Miracles Are A-Maze-ing	_____	☐ Rely on God	_____
☐ Miracle Matchup	_____	☐ Jesus Feeds Thousands of People	_____
☐ Jesus Changes Water to Wine	_____	☐ My "Loaves and Fish"	_____
☐ Jesus' First Miracle	_____	☐ Make a Diorama	_____
☐ Jesus Fills the Net	_____	☐ Jesus Walks on Water	_____
☐ Become a "Fisher of Men"	_____	☐ Would Your Faith Sink or Float?	_____
☐ Make a Sponge Fish	_____	☐ Faith to Float	_____
☐ Make a Boat	_____	☐ Make a String Picture	_____
☐ Caught in a Storm	_____	☐ The Coin in a Fish's Mouth	_____
☐ Tossed About in a Storm	_____	☐ Jesus Withers a Fig Tree	_____
☐ See the Sea	_____	☐ Jesus Fills the Nets Again!	_____
☐ The Missing Word	_____	☐ Play a Fishing Game	_____

Jesus Heals

Palestine, Where Jesus Lived

Draw a line from each miracle to the place on the map where it happened.

1. Jesus heals a leper near Capernaum.

2. Jesus heals a centurion's servant in Capernaum.

3. Jesus brings a widow's son back to life in Nain.

4. Jesus heals Simon Peter's mother-in-law in Capernaum.

5. Jesus sends demons into pigs at Gadara.

6. Jesus heals and forgives sins of a man in Capernaum.

7. Jesus heals a bleeding woman in Capernaum.

8. Jesus brings Jairus's daughter back to life in Capernaum.

9. Jesus heals two blind men in Capernaum.

10. In Capernaum, Jesus heals a man who couldn't speak.

11. In the region of Decapolis, Jesus heals a man who was deaf.

12. Jesus heals a royal official's son in Cana.

13. In Jerusalem, Jesus heals a man who was blind.

14. Jesus heals a blind man in Bethsaida.

15. Jesus heals a boy possessed by a demon near Galilee.

16. In Galilee, Jesus heals a woman who had been crippled.

17. Jesus heals ten lepers in Samaria.

18. In Jerusalem, on the sabbath, Jesus heals a man born blind.

19. Jesus gives sight to blind Bartimaeus in Jericho.

20. Jesus raises Lazarus from the dead in Bethany.

21. Jesus heals Malchus's ear in the Garden of Gethsemane.

MEDITERRANEAN SEA

N

Bethsaida

Capernaum

SEA of GALILEE

Cana

Galilee

Decapolis

Gadara

Nain

Samaria

Jordan River

Jericho

Bethany

Jerusalem

Garden of Gethsemane

DEAD SEA

What did Jesus do with this mud?

You can find the answer on pages 74-75 or in John 9:1-4.

What went through this roof?

You can find the answer on page 58 or in
Matthew 9:1-8; Mark 2:1-12; and Luke 5:17-26.

Sneak Previews

Why is this woman shocked and happy?

You can find the answer on page 54 or in Luke 7:11-18.

What happened to this man's ear?

You can find the answer on page 83 or in Luke 22: 47-51.

What Was Healed?

Look up the Bible passages for each story. Then draw lines from the Bible verses to the parts of the body Jesus healed. The page numbers tell you where to find the stories in this book.

Page 77

Mark 10:46-52

Page 69

Luke 13:10-17

Page 63

Matthew 12:9-13

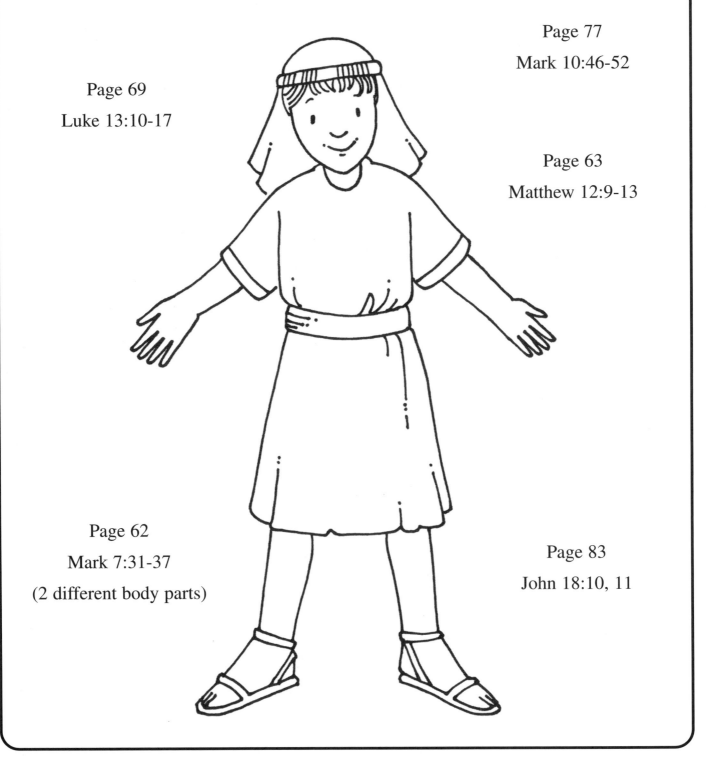

Page 62

Mark 7:31-37

(2 different body parts)

Page 83

John 18:10, 11

Jesus Heals a Leper

Leprosy is a disease that eats away a person's skin. In Jesus' day, there was no medical cure for it. (The word leper *rhymes with* pepper.)

One day a humble man with leprosy saw Jesus and fell on his face before the Lord. "Lord, if you are willing, You can heal me," the man said.

Jesus felt great love for the leper and said, "I am willing. Be well." Right away the man's sores disappeared.

Jesus told the man not to tell anyone he was well. Jesus said to show himself to the priest and offer a gift at the temple. This way, the Jewish leaders would know Jesus had healed him. The man, however, couldn't keep quiet. He told so many people that the news spread like fire.

Fit these words into the puzzle: look, humble, rot, touching.

1. Leprosy was a disease that caused flesh to _____.
2. The leper fell on his face because he was _____.
3. Jesus wasn't disgusted by the man's sores because Jesus loves everyone, no matter what we _____ like.
4. Jesus healed the leper by _____ him and saying for him to be clean.

Suppose you were the one who had leprosy and Jesus healed you. Would it be hard for you to keep it a secret? Why or why not?

Draw a star in this box when you've read the story in *Matthew 8:1-4; Mark 1:40-45; and Luke 5:12-15.*

Jesus Heals a Centurion's Servant

When Jesus entered the city of Capernaum, a centurion (a leader of 100 Roman soldiers) came to Him. "Lord, my servant is sick and is about to die." The centurion cared about his servant and wanted him to get better. Jesus said, "I will come and heal him." But the centurion stopped Him, "Lord, I'm not worthy for You to come to my home, but if You'll only say the word, my servant will be healed. You see I know all about authority. If I say to one of my soldiers, 'Go,' he goes; and to another, 'Come,' he comes, and to my servant, 'Do this,' and he does it. That's why all You have to do is say the word and my servant will be healed." Jesus was amazed when He heard this, and He said to the people following Him, "I haven't found a faith as great as this in all of Israel." Impressed with the centurion's faith, Jesus said to him, "Go your way. Your servant will be healed." That very same hour the servant was healed.

Make a Shield of Faith

Centurions wore armor to protect them in battle. Ephesians 6:13 tells us to wear the full armor of God. Verse 6 says to take up the shield of faith, with which we can put out all the devil's flaming arrows. The centurion used his shield of faith to fight doubts that his servant would be healed.

What You Need

- paper plate
- foil
- permanent marker
- wide masking tape or duct tape
- paper
- pen
- friend

What You Do

1. Cover the paper plate with foil.

2. Write FAITH on it with a permanent marker.

3. Stick two pieces of wide tape together to make a handle. Leave one piece longer on both ends of the other piece so you can stick the handle to the back of your shield.

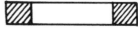

4. On pieces of paper, write doubts the devil gives you about Jesus being able to help you. Crumble them up and have a friend toss them at you while you shield yourself with your faith. Can your faith protect you?

☐ *Draw a star in this box when you've read the story in Matthew 8:5-13 and Luke 7:1-10.*

Jesus Heals Peter's Mother-in-Law

When Jesus went to Simon Peter's house, He saw that the mother of Peter's wife was sick in bed with a fever. Jesus touched her hand and the fever left her. Then she got up and served everyone.

SERVE! It Makes Your Heart Grow!

Right after Peter's mother-in-law was healed, she began helping others. When the Lord helps us, it makes us want to serve. Serving others helps us love them more. *When you do something for someone else today, color in the smallest heart. Each time you serve someone during the day, color in another section of the heart.*

Draw a star in this box when you've read the story in Matthew 8:14, 15; Mark 1:29-31; and Luke 4:38, 39.

Jesus Brings a Window's Son Back to Life

Unscramble the bold words and write them in the blanks that follow. Then read this amazing story.

When Jesus came to the **teag** _____ of the city of Nain, He saw a **aded** _____ man being carried out. This man was the only son of a **wowid** _____ (a woman whose husband had died). When Jesus saw the mother of the dead man, He had compassion (great love) for her and said, "Don't cry." Then He **chedout** _____ the coffin. The **lopepe** _____ carrying the coffin stopped. Jesus said, "Young man, I say to you, arise."

Suddenly, the dead man sat up and began to **kapes** _____ . The people were **mzaade** _____ and praised God saying, "A great prophet is among us" and "God has **sitevid** _____ His people." Throughout Judea and the other regions **drouna** _____ it, the word **wnet** _____ out about **esJsu** _____.

Draw a star in this box when you've read the story in Luke 7:11-18.

With God, Nothing's Impossible

Jesus did what seemed impossible when He raised people from the dead. Some of your problems may seem impossible to solve, but the Lord can do anything. He may not solve our problems right away, but in the long run, He will work things out for our good if we trust Him.

1. Draw a picture of one of your problems in the "before" box.
2. Pray about your problem, and keep praying about it.
3. When the Lord answers your prayer, draw a picture in the "after" box.
Be patient even if it seems like a long time. Remember the Lord hears your prayers and He will help you. Nothing is impossible with God.

BEFORE

AFTER

Jesus Turns a Man's Life Around

Jesus turns people's lives around, like the man in this story. *Use a mirror to turn this story around.*

Once Jesus came across a wild man who lived among graves. The crazy man had often cried and cut himself with stones. No one had been able to calm him, and he broke any chains that were put on him.

Demons were living in the man. Jesus made the demons leave the man and enter pigs. When the demons entered the pigs, the pigs ran down a steep cliff and drowned in the sea.

People who had fed the pigs ran to tell others what had happened. When they returned, they saw that the man who had been crazy was calm, dressed, and normal.

Draw a star in this box when you've read the story in Matthew 8:28-34; Mark 5:1-20; and Luke 8:26-39.

Jesus Raises a Twelve-Year-Old Girl

Read the story and then find at least five things that are different between the two pictures.

Jairus was a ruler of the synagogue, and he was also a father. Right now his twelve-year-old daughter was dying and nothing else mattered to him. Jairus wanted a chance to talk to Jesus. When he found Jesus, Jairus got down on his knees and begged Jesus, "Please come—my only daughter is about to die. Come and lay Your hands on her so she will be healed and will live."

Jesus, however, couldn't come right away because another person wanted healing. Meanwhile, members of Jairus's household arrived and said to Jairus, "Don't bother Jesus anymore. Your daughter is dead." When Jesus heard this, He said to Jairus, "Don't be afraid; just trust Me." Then Jesus left the

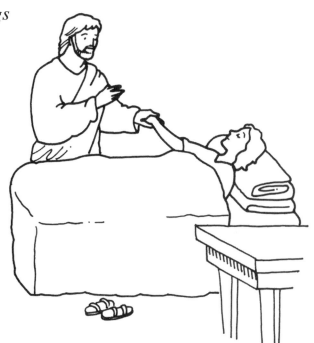

crowd and made His way to Jairus's house. Peter, James, and John went along with Him.

When they arrived, people were weeping and wailing. When Jesus and the apostles entered the house, Jesus asked, "Why are you making all this fuss? The girl isn't dead; she's asleep."

The people laughed at Jesus, but He asked everyone to go outside except Jairus, Jairus's wife, Peter, James, and John. When He went into the room where Jairus's daughter was lying, Jesus took her hand and said, "Little girl, get up." The girl opened her eyes and stood up! Jesus must have been smiling when he turned to her parents and told them to get her something to eat. Jairus and his family were astonished, but Jesus told them not to tell anyone what He had done.

Draw a star in this box when you've read the story in Matthew 9:18, 19, 23-26; and Mark 5:21-23, 35-43.

The Man Through the Roof

The man this story is about is being lowered right through the story itself. Fold the page so the text meets and you can read what happened.

One day Jesus was teaching in a house crowded that four men who wanted get him through the door. The sick So the four carried their friend on a tiles, and lowered the sick man faith, He said, "Son, take heart, your teachers heard this, they were furious. sins," they said among themselves. speaking against God. They refused to Jesus knew what the Jewish teachers say 'Your sins are forgiven' or to say pick up your mat, and walk'? I will forgive sins." Jesus then turned to the pick up your mat, and go home." up his mat, and walked through the were amazed and praised God, "We

in the city of Capernaum. It was so their sick friend to be healed couldn't man was paralyzed and couldn't walk. mat up onto the roof, pulled off some through the roof. When Jesus saw their sins are forgiven." When the Jewish "Only God has the authority to forgive The Jewish teachers thought Jesus was believe that Jesus was God's Son. were thinking and said, "Is it easier to to a man who cannot walk, 'Stand up, show you that I have power on earth to paralyzed man and said, "Stand up, Immediately the man stood up, picked crowd. When the crowd saw this, they have seen remarkable things today."

Draw a star in this box when you've read the story in Matthew 9:1-8; Mark 2:1-12; and Luke 5:17-26.

Bring Your Friends to Jesus

Sin cripples a person's heart just like a disease can cripple a person's body. Jesus knew it was more important for people to be forgiven of sins than to be physically healed. But Jesus healed people because He loved them and wanted them to believe in Him. The man in this story had four friends who brought him to Jesus so he could be healed, both inside and out. How can you be a true friend to someone who doesn't know Jesus?

Write an idea on each step.

Steps I can take to help
_____ know Jesus.
friend's name

Healed by a Touch

Help the sick woman make her way through the crowd to reach Jesus. When you're on the right path, fill in the blanks in the story with the words from the woman's path. These words are in the correct path: twelve, clothes, crowd, stopped, hidden, touched, well

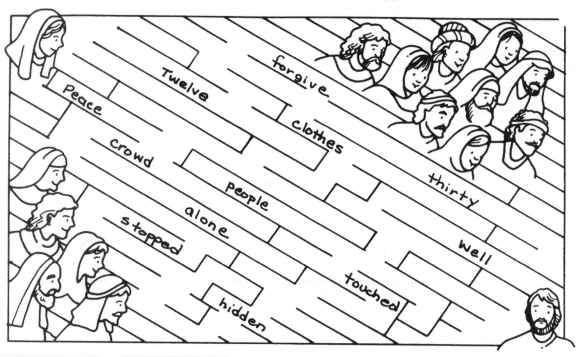

A woman who had been bleeding for_____ years had spent all of her money on doctors, but she was getting worse. When she heard about Jesus, she thought, "If I could just touch His _____, I'll be well."

One day as Jesus was making His way through a _____ , the woman came up behind Jesus and touched the hem of His clothes. Right away her bleeding _____. Jesus said, "Who touched Me?" His disciples said, "The crowd is closed in on You and You want to know who touched You?" Jesus said, "Somebody has touched Me; I can tell that power has gone out of Me."

Jesus looked around and saw the woman. When she knew she wasn't _____ among the crowd, she came out, trembling, and fell down in front of Jesus. The woman then told Him and all the people why she had _____ Jesus and how she had been healed right away.

In a kind voice, Jesus said to her, "Daughter, don't be afraid. Your faith has made you _____. Go in peace."

Draw a star in this box when you've read the story in Matthew 9:20-22; Mark 5:25-34; and Luke 8:43-48.

The Two Blind Men

Two blind men followed Jesus and cried, out, "You Son of David, have mercy on us." King David was Israel's greatest king, and Jesus was from his family line.

Jesus stopped and said, "Do you believe I can heal you?" They said, "Yes, Lord." Then He touched their eyes and said "According to your faith, let it happen to you." And their eyes were opened.

Jesus said, "See that no one knows it." But as soon as they were gone, they spread Jesus' fame throughout that area.

Write in Braille

Today people who are blind read braille—words that are written with raised dots. If this code were actually written in braille, the filled-in circles would be bumps. *Use the braille dots to discover the question Jesus asked the blind men.*

BRAILLE CODE

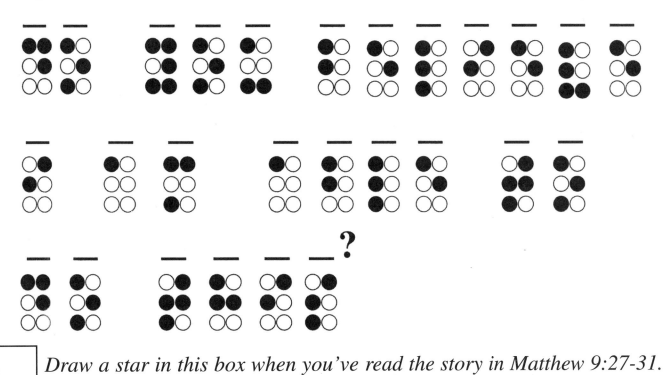

Draw a star in this box when you've read the story in Matthew 9:27-31.

In Plain Speech

A man who couldn't speak was brought to Jesus. After Jesus cast out a demon, the man was able to speak. The crowds were amazed and said, "No one in Israel has ever seen anything like this." The Pharisees (Jewish leaders), however, said Jesus cast out demons with Satan's help. (Of course, that wasn't true.)

Another time, a deaf man who could barely talk was brought to Jesus. Jesus took the man away from the crowd. He put His fingers in the man's ears, spit, and then touched the man's tongue. Then Jesus looked up to heaven and said, "Ephphatha!" (which means "Be opened!"). Immediately, the man could hear and speak plainly.

Mum's the Word

Get together with a friend and pretend that neither of you can talk. Think of other ways you could "talk" to each other. For example, you could write notes or make hand motions. Whatever you do, don't make any noise or sounds.

How long did you go without talking? Life would be pretty tough if you couldn't speak or hear, wouldn't it? Imagine how glad the men in these stories were when Jesus healed them!

□ *Draw a star in this box when you've read the story in Matthew 9:32-34; Mark 7:31-37.*

Jesus Heals a Man's Hand

One sabbath, as Jesus taught in the synagogue, a man whose right hand was shriveled and useless was there listening to Him. The Jewish leaders believed it was wrong to heal people on the sabbath, and they were hoping to catch Jesus breaking the sabbath. Jesus knew what they were thinking and told the man with the shriveled hand to stand up.

Jesus asked the people there, "If you have a sheep that falls into a pit on the sabbath, wouldn't you grab it and lift it out? A man is more valuable than a sheep. Is it wrong to do good on the sabbath?"

Jesus looked at them and felt very sad that the people's hearts were hard. Then He told the man to hold out his shriveled hand. When the man did, it looked just as perfect as his other hand!

A 'Hand'-y Reminder

Sunday is a good day for doing extra things for God. In fact, any day is a good day for that, but let's make Sunday a special time of doing good. Each Sunday, pray and ask God how to show you ways to serve Him. Make a list of things to do on your notepad and check them off as you do them.

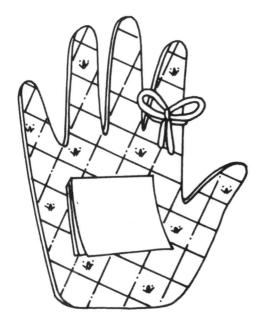

What You Need

- a square of self-adhesive paper bigger than your hand
- a square of thick cardboard bigger than your hand
- a pen
- tape (duct tape works well)
- a paper clip
- a small sticky notepad (or make one by stapling about 25 small squares of paper together)
- glue
- a ribbon or string

What You Do

1. *Trace the outline of your hand onto the self-adhesive paper*
2. *Remove its backing and stick it onto the cardboard.*
3. *Cut out the handprint.*
4. *Glue the notepad to the palm of the hand. Let it dry well.*
5. *Make a loop for hanging by taping the paper clip to the back of the handprint.*
6. *Tie a bow around the index finger to remind you to do good things on Sunday and every other day of the week, too!*

Draw a star in this box when you've read the story in Matthew 12:9-13; Mark 3:1-5; and Luke 6:6-11.

A Royal Healing

Color this picture.

A royal official (a person who worked for the king) went to see Jesus in Cana. The official asked Jesus to heal his dying son. Jesus said, "Unless you see miracles, you won't believe." The official, however, did believe Jesus and replied, "Sir, come or my child will die." Jesus said, "Go on your way. Your son will live." Later the man found out that his son had begun to get well and his fever had left him at about one o'clock in the afternoon, the same time that Jesus had said that the son would live. The man and his whole household believed.

Draw a star in this box when you've read the story in John 4:46-54.

Make a Special Journal

Does God do miracles in your life? People who trust God can see Him doing a lot of wonderful things in their lives every day. Spend time with someone who loves God. Ask that person to tell you about some things God has done for him or her. To help you remember what God is doing for you, make a journal to record the wonderful things God does in your life.

What You Need

- file folder
- scissors
- fabric scrap about 10" x 13"
- glue or glue stick
- about 42 inches colored piping (a fabric notion) or gathered lace
- masking tape
- markers
- about 10 sheets of typing paper
- paper hole punch
- about 1/2 yard ribbon or gold cord

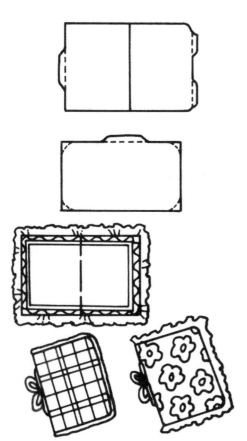

What You Do

1. *Cut the folder in half, and throw away the half with the tab cut out of it. Cut the tab off the other half to make a rectangle. Round off the corners, too.*

2. *Spread a thin, even coat of glue on one side of the rectangle and cover it with fabric. Fold the extra fabric over and glue it to the other side of the rectangle.*

3. *Glue the piping or lace to the back (uncovered side) to make a border that will show on the fabric-covered side. Cover the edges of the piping or lace with a strip of masking tape. If you'd like, use the markers to decorate the tape.*

4. *Center the typing paper on the uncovered side of the rectangle. Carefully fold the rectangle and paper in half. Punch a hole through both the typing paper and rectangle in the crease about 2 1/2 inches from the top edge. Punch another hole 2 1/2 inches from the bottom edge.*

5. *Thread the ribbon or cord through the holes and tie a bow on the fabric-covered side. Make a good crease so your journal will open and close easily.*

A Blind Man Healed in Bethsaida

Color the picture using the code.

COLORING CODE

R=RED   B=BLUE
Y=YELLOW   P=PURPLE
O=ORANGE   BN=BROWN
LG=LIGHT GREEN   DG=DARK GREEN

When Jesus went to Bethsaida, some people brought a blind man to Him and asked Jesus to heal him. Jesus took the blind man by the hand and led him out of the town. After He spit on the man's eyes, Jesus put His hands upon the man and asked if he could see. The man looked up and said, "I see men. They look like walking trees."

Jesus put His hands on the man's eyes again and had him look up. The man could see everyone clearly. Jesus sent the man to his house and told him not to go into the town nor to tell it to anyone in the town.

Draw a star in this box when you've read the story in Mark 8:22-26.

A Healing at the Pool of Bethesda

By the sheep market in Jerusalem, there was a pool called Bethesda. This pool had five porches around it. A lot of sick people lay on the porches, waiting for the water to move. Many people believed that an angel would go into the pool and move the water. Whoever stepped into the pool right after the water moved would be healed.

Now, a man who had been sick for thirty-eight years was lying there. Jesus saw him one sabbath and knew the man had been there a long time. Jesus asked, "Do you want to get well?" The man said, "Whenever the water moves, I don't have anyone to put me into the pool. Someone always steps down before me."

Jesus said to him, "Rise! Pick up your mat and walk." Right away the man was healed. He picked up his mat and walked.

Later, some of the Jewish leaders told this man it was against the law to carry mats on the sabbath. The healed man said, "The man who made me well told me to carry it." They asked who it was, but the healed man didn't know Jesus' name.

Later Jesus saw the healed man in the temple and told him not to sin anymore. The man left and told the Jews it was Jesus who had healed him. Because of this, the Jews were angry at Jesus and wanted to kill Him.

Bethesda Tic-Tac-Toe

If a statement is right, draw an "o" over it. If it's wrong, draw an "x" over it.
If you're correct, you will have three x's or o's in a row.

The people thought the first one to step into the pool after an angel stirred the waters would be healed.	The sick man's mat was too heavy for him to carry.	The healed man told the Jewish leaders he didn't know who made him well.
The people thought an angel would stir the water at the pool of Bethesda.	It was against the law to carry a mat on the sabbath.	When the healed man learned Jesus' name, he kept it a secret to protect Jesus.
The man Jesus healed had been sick for 52 years.	The healed man blamed the person who healed him for causing him to break the sabbath.	The Jewish leaders wanted to kill Jesus for healing on the sabbath.

☐ *Draw a star in this box when you've read the story in John 5:2-16.*

Jesus Heals a Young Boy

For each picture, cross out the letters that spell its name. The leftover letters make up other words. Next, write the words in the blanks of the story. When all the blanks are filled, read the story from start to finish. The first puzzle is done for you.

1. AJIESRPLANUSE

2. DBIISTKUREBED

3. RFABOBIATMS

4. BFAANIANTHA

5. BBEALTIHETVUBE

6. CDLEAOCDK

7. CSTAKOEOD

8. SHALELOLNE

9. PRCAYOEWR

A man brought his only child to 1. ___Jesus___. The man said, "Please have mercy on my son. He has had seizures since he was a child, and is often very 2. _____. He 3. _____ at the mouth and hurts himself. You can do anything. Please have compassion on us and help us."

Jesus said the people needed to have 4. _____. He said, "If you can 5. _____, all things are possible to those who believe."

Jesus said, "You dumb and deaf evil spirit, I command you to come out of him and stay out of him." The boy seemed to be 6. _____, but when Jesus took his hand, the boy 7. _____.

When the disciples were 8. _____ with Jesus, they asked why they hadn't been able to get rid of the bad spirit when they had tried earlier. Jesus said that kind of faith came only by 9. _____ and fasting (not eating).

☐ *Draw a star in this box when you've read the story in Matthew 17:14-21; Mark 9:14-29; and Luke 9:37-43.*

Jesus Heals a Woman's Back

One day while Jesus was teaching in a synagogue (Jewish church), on the sabbath, He saw a woman who had been sick for eighteen years. Her illness had crippled her and she was bent over. Jesus said to her, "Woman, you are free from your illness," and He laid His hands on her. Right away she stood up straight and glorified God.

The ruler of the synagogue was angry because Jesus had healed on the sabbath, which was against the law. He said to the people, "There are six days in which men work. Come to be healed during those days, not on the sabbath."

Jesus replied, "You hypocrite (someone who pretends to be good when he really isn't). Don't you take your ox or donkey from its stall and lead it to water on the sabbath? Shouldn't this woman whom Satan has bound for eighteen years be made free on the sabbath?" When He had said these things, the people against Him were ashamed, while others rejoiced about the great things He did.

Do You Want to Be Flexible?

Sometimes we get set in our ways, but if we learn to bend and be flexible, the Lord can straighten out our hearts and attitudes, like He straightened the woman in this story. Be willing to let the Lord make you the way He wants you to be.

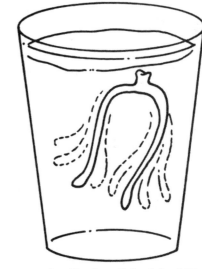

If you put a chicken bone in vinegar and change the vinegar twice a week, the bone will become flexible in two to three weeks. As you wait for the bone to become flexible, work at becoming more flexible yourself.

☐ *Draw a star in this box when you've read the story in Luke 13:10-17.*

Healing in a Pharisee's House

One sabbath, Jesus went to eat at a Jewish leader's house. There, He saw a man with dropsy. This was a disease that made the man swell up with too much fluid.

Jesus asked, "Is it legal to heal on the sabbath?" The leaders didn't say anything. Jesus took hold of the man, healed him, and let him go. Then Jesus said, "If your donkey or ox fell into a hole on the sabbath, wouldn't you immediately pull it out?"

Pull the oxen out of the hole. If their words fit the puzzle, put the words in the blanks to find what Jesus was trying to tell the Jewish leaders.

Doing _____ _____ _____

always _____ _____ .

Draw a star in this box when you've read the story in Luke 14:1-6.

Some people would have helped their animals on the sabbath, but they didn't want Jesus to help a sick person. They cared more about donkeys and oxen than a man! Would you treat an animal better than a person?

Fill in this chart to find out.

Pets and People

Your Pet

Would you give him a piece?

☐ Yes ☐ No

Your Family

Would you share?

☐ Yes ☐ No

Do you show love to your pet?

☐ Yes ☐ No

Do you show love to your family?

☐ Yes ☐ No

Would you comfort your pet?

☐ Yes ☐ No

Would you comfort your brother or sister?

☐ Yes ☐ No

Do you play with your pet?

☐ Yes ☐ No

Do you play with your brother or sister?

☐ Yes ☐ No

The Ten Lepers

Put the letters that are missing from the story into the blanks of the message at the bottom of this page to find something this story teaches.

As Jesus wa_ on His way to Jerusalem, He passed through a vill_ge in Samaria. Men who were lepers met Him there and stood far awa_ from Him. _hey yelled, "Jesus, Master, _ave mercy on us." Jesus told them to go show themselves to the priests. _s they we_t, they were healed.

When one of them realized he was healed, he turned bac_ and praised God with a loud voice. Then he fell down on hi_ face at Jesus' fee_, giving Him thanks. Jesus said, "Weren't ten cleansed? Where are the nine? _nly this one stran_er has returned t_ give glory to God. Stand up and go your way; your faith has ma_e you whole."

___ __ ___ _____ __ ___ __ ___.

The Message

Say Thanks

Every day the Lord blesses us and answers our prayers. Sometimes we forget to thank Him for what He has done, just like nine of the lepers. *Connect the dots and unscramble things for which you can be thankful. Be sure to thank the Lord for them.*

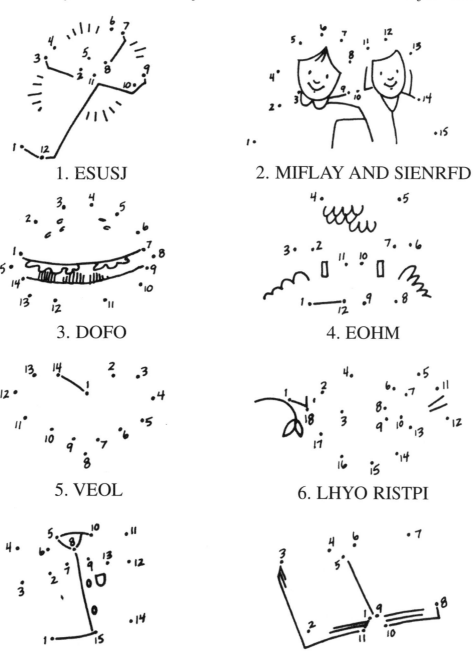

1. ESUSJ

2. MIFLAY AND SIENRFD

3. DOFO

4. EOHM

5. VEOL

6. LHYO RISTPI

7. STHECLO

8. LBEIB

Draw a star in this box when you've read the story in Luke 17:11-19.

A Blind Man Healed with Clay

The man in the story had something wrong with his eyes. This story is missing its I's. *Return the letter I to the story.*

One sabbath when Jesus saw a man who had been bl_nd s_nce b_rth, H_s d_sc_ples asked _f the bl_ndness was caused by s_n of the man or h_s parents. Jesus sa_d ne_ther. He was l_ke th_s so the works of God could be shown through h_m. Jesus sp_t on the ground, made clay from the sp_ttle, and put the clay on the man's eyes. Then He sa_d, "Go wash _n the Pool of S_loam." The man went and washed. When he returned, he could see.

People who knew the man had been bl_nd took h_m to the Phar_sees (Jew_sh leaders). The Phar_sees sa_d, "Jesus _s not of God because He doesn't keep the sabbath day." Others sa_d, "How can a s_nner do such m_racles?" They asked the healed man what he thought of Jesus. He sa_d, "He _s a prophet."

The Jews asked the healed man's parents _f he had really been bl_nd and how he could see. The parents sa_d he had been bl_nd but the Jews should ask the son how h_s eyes had opened. They were afra_d to say _t was Jesus because the Jews had agreed that anyone who sa_d Jesus was the Chr_st would be put out of the church. The Jews called the healed man _n aga_n and sa_d, "G_ve God the pra_se; we know Jesus _s a s_nner." The healed man sa_d, "_ know _ was bl_nd and now _ see."

The Jews sa_d, "You're Jesus' d_sc_ple, but we're Moses' d_sc_ples. We know God spoke to Moses. We don't know where th_s man comes from."

The healed man sa_d, "Here _s an _ncred_ble th_ng. You don't know where He comes from, yet He has opened my eyes. Now we know God doesn't hear s_nners, but God hears anyone who worsh_ps H_m and does what He wants h_m to do. S_nce the world began, no one heard of anyone open_ng the eyes of someone born bl_nd. _f th_s man wasn't of God, He couldn't do anyth_ng."

The Jews sa_d to h_m, "You were born _n s_n and you teach us?" And they threw h_m out.

When Jesus heard the man had been thrown out of the synagogue, He found h_m and sa_d, "Do you bel_eve _n the Son of God?" The man answered, "Who _s He that _ m_ght bel_eve _n H_m?" Jesus sa_d, "You've seen H_m and _t's H_m that talks w_th you." The man sa_d, "Lord, _ bel_eve" and he worsh_ped Jesus.

☐ *Draw a star in this box when you've read the story in John 9:1-41.*

Physical and Spiritual Eye Chart

If you believe what the chart says, your spiritual eyes are in good shape. If you can read the bottom line from five feet away, your physical eyes are in good shape, too, and you have 20/20 vision.

I
SEE
THAT
JESUS
IS THE SON OF
GOD AND IS MY
SAVIOR.

Blind Bartimaeus

This story will have a happy ending if you put the correct endings on the words. The endings form a border around the story, and each ending belongs on only one word.

• eive • aith

• sus
• ing
• way
• gan

• aise
• ood
• fort
• ind

When Je___ and His disciples were leav___ Jericho, a blind man named Bartimaeus sat begging by the high___. When he heard that Jesus of Nazareth was passing by, he be___ to cry out, "Jesus, Son of David, have mercy on me." People told the man he should be qu___, but he cried even louder, "You Son of David, have me___ on me."

Jesus stop___ walking and told some people to bring Bartimaeus to Him. They said to the bl___ man, "Take com____. Stand up; He's calling for you." And he st___ and went to Jesus.

Jesus said, "What do you want me to do to you?" The blind man said, "I want to rec____ my sight."

Jesus said, "Go your way; your f____ has made you whole." Right away Bartimaeus received his s____ and followed Jesus, glorifying God. And when all the people saw it, they gave pr____ to God.

• ped • rcy • iet • ple • ight •

Draw a star in this box when you've read the story in Matthew 20:29-34; Mark 10:46-52; and Luke 18:35-43.

Praise God with a Poem

When Bartimaeus and others were healed by Jesus, they praised God. Praising God is expressing how great you think He is. You can praise Him many different ways. One way is to talk about His goodness. Some others are to pray about it, sing about it, and write about it. Praise the Lord right now by writing a five-line poem called a *cinquain*.

Here's an example:

Lord.
Compassionate. Powerful.
Healing. Teaching. Saving.
I praise your name.
Jesus.

Fill in the blanks:

_____

1 noun (person, place, or thing)

_____ _____

2 adjectives (describing words)

_____ _____ _____

3 vesrbs (action words)

_____ _____ _____ _____

4 word sentence

_____

1 noun renaming first noun

Lazarus Returns to Life: A Puppet Show

What You Need

- puppets from page 81
- scissors
- tape
- craft sticks or spoons
- shoe box
- clay
- flat rock
- paper or fabric (optional)

What You Do

1. *Cut out each puppet and tape it to a Popsicle stick or the handle of a spoon.*

2. *Cut a long slit in the bottom of a plain shoe box. Cover the box with paper or fabric, if desired.*

3. *Make a tomb by molding clay on a cup. Peel the clay off the cup. Make an entrance in the clay cave and place a flat rock in front of it.*

4. *Turn the box upside down. Stick the puppets up through the slit. Have them act out the story as someone reads it aloud. Leave Lazarus inside the cave until the end of the story.*

Narrator: Mary and Martha, who lived in Bethany, sent a message to Jesus that their brother Lazarus was about to die.

Jesus: It is for the glory of God and so the Son of God will be glorified.

Narrator: Jesus loved Martha, Mary, and Lazarus, but after He had heard Lazarus was sick, He stayed two days where He was. Then He said to His disciples . . .

Jesus: Let's go to Judea again.

Disciples: Master, lately the Jews tried to kill You with stones and You plan to go there again?

Jesus: Our friend Lazarus sleeps; I go to wake him.

Disciples: If he sleeps, it will help him get well.

Narrator: They didn't know Jesus meant Lazarus was dead and Jesus would bring him back to life.

Jesus: Lazarus is dead. I'm glad for your sakes that I wasn't there because this will help you believe. Let us go to him.

Thomas Didymus *(to the other disciples)*: Let us go, too, that we may die with Him.

Narrator: They traveled a little less than two miles and when Jesus arrived, He found out that Lazarus had been in his grave four days already. Many people had come to comfort Mary and Martha. When Martha heard Jesus was on His way, she ran to meet Him but Mary stayed in the house. When Martha saw Jesus, she said,

Martha: If You had been here my brother would not have died. But I know that even now, whatever You ask of God, He will give it to You.

Jesus: Your brother will rise again.

Martha: I know he will rise in the resurrection at the last day.

Jesus: I am the resurrection and the life. He that believes in Me, though he were dead, yet he will live. Whoever lives and believes in Me will never die. Do you believe this?

Martha: Yes, Lord. I believe You're the Christ, the Son of God who would come into the world.

Narrator: Then Martha went to get Mary. Mary came quickly to see Jesus. When she reached Him, she fell down at His feet and said . . .

Mary: Lord, if You had been here, my brother would not have died.

Narrator: When Jesus saw her weeping and others with her weeping, He groaned inside and was troubled.

Jesus: Where have you laid him?

Mary: Come and see.

Narrator: Jesus wept, and the Jews said . . .

Jews: See how He loved him. Couldn't this man who opened the eyes of the blind have kept this man from dying?

Narrator: Jesus felt bad as He came to the grave. The tomb was a cave and there was a stone upon it.

Jesus: Take away the stone.

Martha: Lord, by now he stinks; he's been dead four days.

Jesus: Didn't I say to you that if you would believe, you would see the glory of God?

Narrator: Then they took away the stone from the place where Lazarus was. Jesus lifted up His eyes and said . . .

Jesus: I thank You that You have heard me. And I knew You always hear me, but I said it so the people standing here would believe that You sent me.

Narrator: Then Jesus called out loudly

Jesus: Lazarus, come forth.

Narrator: Lazarus, who had been dead, came out wrapped with grave clothes. His face was covered with a napkin.

Jesus: Unwrap him and let him go.

Narrator: Many of the Jews who saw what Jesus did believed in Him. Others went to the Jewish church leaders and told them what Jesus had done. The leaders were afraid the people would follow Jesus instead of them, and they began to plan how to kill Jesus.

Draw a star in this box when you've read the story in John 11:1-53.

Tell the Story with Puppets

Jesus

Disciples

Mary

Martha

Jewish
Leaders

Lazarus

The Servant's Ear

The leaders of the Jews had decided to kill Jesus and they needed Judas Iscariot (one of Jesus' disciples) to take them to Jesus. Judas would identify Jesus with a kiss.

While Jesus and the other disciples were in the Garden of Gethsemane, Judas and a crowd approached. As Judas was about to kiss Jesus, Jesus said, "Are you going to betray Me with a kiss?"

When the disciples who were with Jesus saw what was happening, they asked, "Lord, should we strike them with our swords?" Simon Peter cut off the right ear of the high priest's servant, Malchus. Jesus said, "Let them do this for now." Then He touched Malchus's ear and healed it.

Learning to Forgive

	JESUS	ME
The Situation	People were trying to take Jesus away and kill Him.	*A way someone has or might try to hurt me:* _____
The Response	The natural feeling when someone hurts you might be to hurt them back. But Jesus didn't. In fact, when Peter defended Him by cutting off the servant's ear, Jesus healed it.	*How Jesus would want me to act:* _____ _____ _____ _____

☐ *Draw a star in this box when you've read the story in Matthew 26:51-54; Mark 14:47; and John 18:10-11.*

In My Daily Life

Fill in the blanks.

If I feel like my problems are impossible to fix . . .

I can remember that no problem is too difficult for Jesus. Jairus's 1. _____ (p. 57), the widow's 2. _____ (p. 54), and 3. _____ (p. 79) were dead, but Jesus brought them back to life.

If I feel like being mean to someone who has hurt me . . .

I can try to love them the way Jesus did when He replaced the ear of the high priest's 4. _____ (p. 83). Malchus wanted Jesus to be killed, but Jesus healed him when someone cut off his ear.

If I start to think I'm better than other people . . .

I can remember that Jesus loves us all the same, and I can ask Him to help others the way the 5. _____ (p. 52) asked Jesus to heal his sick servant.

When the Lord blesses me . . .

I can try to be like the one out of 6. _____ _____ (p. 72) and thank Him.

I Did It!

COMPLETED	DATE	COMPLETED	DATE
☐ Sneak Previews	_____	☐ A Royal Healing	_____
☐ What Was Healed?	_____	☐ A Blind Man Healed in Bethsaida	_____
☐ Jesus Heals a Leper	_____	☐ A Healing at the Pool of Bethesda	_____
☐ Jesus Heals a Centurion's Servant	_____	☐ Jesus Heals a Young Boy	_____
☐ Jesus Heals Peter's Mother-in-Law	_____	☐ Jesus Heals a Woman's Back	_____
☐ Jesus Brings a Widow's Son Back to Life	_____	☐ Healing in a Pharisee's House	_____
☐ With God, Nothing's Impossible	_____	☐ The Ten Lepers	_____
☐ Jesus Turns a Man's Life Around	_____	☐ A Blind Man Healed with Clay	_____
☐ Jesus Raises a Twelve-Year-Old Girl	_____	☐ Physical and Spiritual Eye Chart	_____
☐ The Man Through the Roof	_____	☐ Blind Bartimaeus	_____
☐ Bring Your Friends to Jesus	_____	☐ Praise God with a Poem	_____
☐ Healed by a Touch	_____	☐ Lazarus Returns to Life: A Puppet Show	_____
☐ The Two Blind Men	_____	☐ Tell the Story with Puppets	_____
☐ In Plain Speech	_____	☐ The Servant's Ear	_____
☐ Jesus Heals a Man's Hand	_____	☐ In My Daily Life	_____

Jesus Teaches Me to Pray

Riddles about Jesus' Prayers

Fill in the blanks with the correct rhyming words.
You can find the answers by looking up the Bible verses.

1. It rhymes with play. Jesus prayed before it began. It was the _____.
   Mark 1:35

2. It rhymes with fountain. Jesus prayed all night on it. It was a _____.
   Luke 6:12

3. It rhymes with sweeter. Jesus prayed for this man's faith. His name was _____.
   Luke 22:31-34

4. It rhymes with ranks. Before feeding 5,000 people, Jesus gave _____.
   Matthew 14:19

5. It rhymes with earring. Before raising Lazarus, Jesus thanked God for _____.
   John 11:41, 42

6. It rhymes with lids. When asked to pray for them, Jesus welcomed these _____.
   Matthew 19:13-15

7. It rhymes with breath. Moses and Elijah told Jesus about His upcoming _____.
   Luke 9:28-36

8. It rhymes with chill. In Gethsemane, Jesus said He would do God's _____.
   Matthew 26:36-46

9. It rhymes with toss. Jesus prayed for those who killed Him on the _____.
   Luke 23:34

A Message to Decode

Change each letter to the letter that follows it in the alphabet. Change Z to A.

Idrtr snnj shld sn oqzx, zmc rn rgntkc vd.

_____

_____

☐ *Draw a star in this box when you've read the Bible verses listed above.*

Prayer Pillowcase

Decorate a pillowcase to remind yourself to pray before you go to sleep at night and when you wake up in the morning.

What You Need

- permission from a parent
- a pillowcase (sewn from inexpensive muslin or purchased)
- a pencil
- cardboard
- waterproof markers or fabric paint pens

What You Do

1. Draw a moon and write "Jesus prayed at night and so do I" in pencil on one side of your pillowcase.

2. Turn over your pillowcase. Now draw a sun and write "Jesus prayed in the morning and so do I."

3. Put the cardboard inside your pillowcase to make sure that the ink or paint doesn't come through onto the other side.

4. Go over the pencil marks with your favorite colors in permanent markers or fabric paint pens. When it dries you will have a great way to remind yourself to pray every day!

The Lord's Prayer

Jesus liked to pray. One day after He prayed, His disciples asked Him to teach them to pray. What Jesus taught them is called "The Lord's Prayer." This prayer is an example of what our prayers need to be like. Once you know it, you can use it to remind you of things to talk about with God.

You can use the bath stickers on the next page to help you learn the Lord's Prayer. After you take a bath, color the words on this page that you have memorized.

Our Father in heaven,
hallowed be your name,
your kingdom come,
your will be done on earth
as it is in heaven.
Give us today our daily bread.
Forgive us our debts,
as we also have forgiven our
debtors.
And lead us not into temptation,
but deliver us from the evil one.
For yours is the kingdom,
and the power
and the glory for ever. Amen.

☐ *Draw a star in this box when you have memorized Matthew 6:9-13 and read Luke 11:1-4.*

Memorization Bath Stickers

You can use these stickers to learn parts of the Lord's Prayer when you take a bath. Water will hold them to the tiles of the bathtub wall.

What You Need

- gift wrap or construction paper
- cookie cutters (optional)
- pencil
- scissors
- marking pen
- clear adhesive vinyl (such as self-adhesive paper)
- plastic basket (that held strawberries or other fruit)

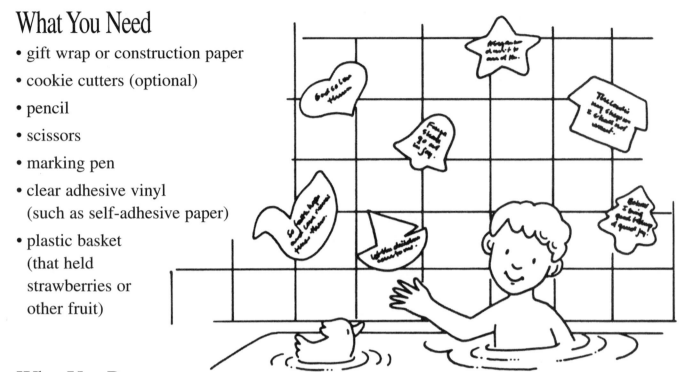

What You Do

1. *Use a pencil to draw 13 shapes or trace around cookie cutters to make 13 shapes on gift wrap or construction paper.*

2. *Cut out the shapes.*

3. *Write one line from the Lord's Prayer on each of the shapes. (You can find the lines on page 91 of this book.)*

4. *Lay a piece of clear adhesive vinyl on a table. Peel off the paper backing.*

5. *Arrange the cut-out shapes on the adhesive vinyl about an inch apart. Remove the paper backing from another piece of adhesive vinyl and put it sticky side down on top of the shapes. Smooth out any bubbles or folds with your hand.*

6. *Cut out the shapes, leaving a 1/2-inch border around each one. Pinch the vinyl edges around each shape to make sure water won't get in.*

7. *When you get the shapes wet, they will stick to the tiles above your tub. Now you can learn the Lord's Prayer when you take a bath!*

8. *Store the bath stickers in a plastic basket.*

Hallowed Be Your Name

When Jesus taught His disciples the Lord's Prayer, He said to pray to God, our Father, "hallowed be your name." That means "Your name is holy." Jesus was showing us that it's good to praise God (say things about His goodness) when we pray.

Fill in the blanks below. Praise God for these things when you pray today.

Something beautiful God created in nature.

_____

Something about God that you think is great.

_____

Something God has done for you or someone you love.

_____

God's Name Is Holy

God, our Father in heaven, wants us to treat His name with respect. We should only use it when we are talking about Him or to Him. Never say "God" or "Lord" as slang or a cuss word.

Can you remember what one of the Ten Commandments says about God's name? (Exodus 20:7)

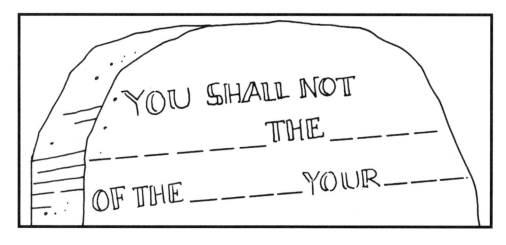

YOU SHALL NOT
_____ THE _ _ _ _ _
OF THE _ _ _ _ _ YOUR _ _ _ _

☐ *Draw a star in this box when you've read Exodus 20:7; and Matthew 6:9.*

Your Will Be Done

Jesus came to earth to do what God the Father wanted Him to do. He said we need to pray for what God wants, too. God knows what's best for you, and if you ask Him He will tell you what He wants you to do.

If you listen carefully when you pray and throughout the day, the Holy Spirit will tell you what God's will is for you. You probably won't hear Him with your ears, but when He speaks to your spirit you will know what He wants you to do. He might also use a Bible verse or another person. However your answers come, you can be sure they are from God if they match what the Bible says.

Let God Be the Pilot

If your life were an airplane, who would be the pilot? You or God? Make this airplane to remind yourself to let God control your life.

What You Need

• 8 1/2 x 11 sheet of paper

• pen

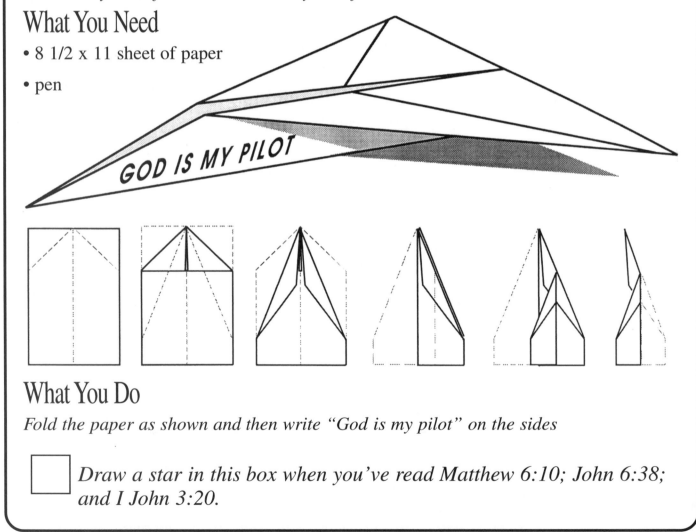

What You Do

Fold the paper as shown and then write "God is my pilot" on the sides

Draw a star in this box when you've read Matthew 6:10; John 6:38; and I John 3:20.

Our Daily Bread

Jesus said we should pray, "Give us today our daily bread." Everything that we need, including food, comes from God.

God fed Elijah in the Old Testament by sending birds to bring him food. He fed Moses and the children of Israel by dropping manna out of heaven. Even if your food doesn't come to you in an amazing way, it still comes to you from God.

Paint Your Daily Bread

Paint "God gave me this bread" on a slice of bread using the egg "paint." On other slices of bread, paint pictures of blessings God has given you.

What You Need

- white bread
- clean paintbrush
- 1 egg
- 4 paper cups
- red and blue food coloring
- spoon
- grown-up help, if needed

What You Do

1. *Wash your hands.*

2. *Separate the egg yolk from the white (you may want to ask a grown-up to help). Crack the egg. Hold your hand over a cup and carefully drop the white and yolk into your hand. Let the white fall through your fingers and you'll be left holding the yolk.*

3. *Drop the yolk into cup number two. Stir the yolk and spoon half of it into cup number three. Pour half of the egg white into the last empty cup.*

4. *Now you can make red, yellow, blue, and green egg paint. One cup with yolk in it is already yellow. Add one drop of blue to the other cup with yolk. Stir and watch it turn green. Add one drop of blue to a cup with egg white and stir. Add one drop of red to the other cup with egg white and stir.*

5. *Paint "God gave me this bread" on a slice of bread using a clean paintbrush and some egg paint. On other slices of bread, you can paint pictures of blessings that God has given you.*

6. *With the help of a grown-up, bake the painted slices in a toaster oven or microwave oven until the egg is dry. Make sandwiches out of the slices.*

Draw a star in this box when you've read Exodus 16:4, 31, 35; I Kings 17:6; and Matthew 6:11.

God Will Feed You

Jesus said that there are more important things to think about than what you eat, drink, and wear. God will give you what you need. He takes care of the birds and you're worth much more than they are! Pray for the things you need, and have faith that God will give them to you.

Jesus said, "Look at the birds of the air; they do not sow or reap or store away in barns, and yet your heavenly Father feeds them. Are you not much much more valuable than they?"

Cut a bird like the one shown from cardboard. Draw eyes and a beak on its face. Tape pennies behind the wings. Try to balance the bird on your finger and make it fly!

Worm Desserts

What You Need

- flat lollipops
- construction paper
- scissors
- a pen
- masking tape
- small flowerpots
- plastic food wrap
- pudding
- chocolate cookie crumbs
- gummy worms

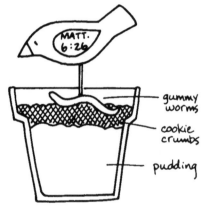

gummy worms

cookie crumbs

pudding

What You Do

1. *Wrap a piece of masking tape around the top of each flowerpot. Write on the tape "God feeds the birds, and He'll always feed me."*
2. *Draw birds and wings on construction paper and cut them out. Write "Matthew 6:26" on the wings. Tape the wings onto the birds and the birds onto the lollipops. Now tape each lollipop stick and bird to the inside of a flowerpot.*
3. *Line each flowerpot with a piece of plastic food wrap.*
4. *Fill the flowerpots nearly to the top with pudding. Put a gummy worm on top of the pudding.*
5. *Cover the top of the pudding with cookie crumbs to look like dirt. Make sure to leave part of the worms showing!*
6. *While you and your family or classmates are eating the desserts, talk about how faithfully God takes care of you.*

☐ *Draw a star in this box when you've read Matthew 6:25, 26.*

God Will Clothe You

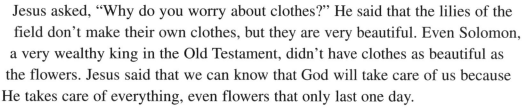

Jesus asked, "Why do you worry about clothes?" He said that the lilies of the field don't make their own clothes, but they are very beautiful. Even Solomon, a very wealthy king in the Old Testament, didn't have clothes as beautiful as the flowers. Jesus said that we can know that God will take care of us because He takes care of everything, even flowers that only last one day.

As you make these flower projects, think about how beautifully God dresses the flowers and how He takes even better care of you.

Flower Picture

What You Need
- flowers
- wax paper
- a heavy book
- clear self-adhesive paper
- jar lid
- marking pen
- scissors
- hole punch
- satin ribbon

What You Do

1. *Arrange some flowers on a piece of wax paper. Cover them with another piece of wax paper and put them inside a heavy book. Don't touch them for a week.*
2. *Make a circle on the self-adhesive paper by tracing around the jar lid with the marking pen. Cut out the circle.*
3. *Peel the backing off the circle. Arrange the flowers on the sticky side.*
4. *Cut a piece of self-adhesive paper bigger than the circle. Peel the backing off of this piece. Put it sticky side down on top of the circle and flowers. Trim off the edges to match the circle.*
5. *Punch a hole near the top of the circle. String the ribbon through the hole and tie a bow. Hang your picture by a thread in a shady window (strong sunlight makes the colors fade).*

Dandelion Necklace or Crown

What You Need
- dandelions

What You Do

1. *Cut a slit in a dandelion's stem with your fingernail.*
2. *Pull the next dandelion's stem through the slit in the stem of the first dandelion.*
3. *Repeat with more dandelions until the necklace will fit on or over your head.*
4. *Make the slit in the last dandelion's stem longer. Carefully pull the first dandelion's blossom through the slit to close your necklace.*

Draw a star in this box when you've read Matthew 6:28-30.

Don't Worry

Jesus asked, "Who of you by worrying can add a single hour to his life?" The answer is a big no one! You can't control that, God does. God has control over everything. Jesus told us not to worry about things like food and clothes and how long we will live. If we think about how to follow God, He will take care of everything else. We can't change things by worrying any more than we can make ourselves grow taller. That's God's job!

Stature Stilts

These stilts can remind you that God is in control.

What You Need

- a grown-up to help
- 2 large empty tin cans with plastic lids
- a can opener
- 2 pieces of twine (each about 24 inches long)
- tape
- 2 index cards
- pen

What You Do

1. *Turn the cans upside-down. Use the can opener to make a hole on each side of what are now the tops of the cans.*

2. *Remove the plastic lids. Ask a grown-up to thread a piece of twine through the holes. IMPORTANT: Don't try this yourself. The sharp edges inside the can could cut you. Replace the plastic lids.*

3. *Write "Stilts can make me higher," on one index card. Tape the card to a can.*

4. *Write on the other card "but only God can make me taller." Tape it to the other can.*

5. *Stand on the cans and have a grown-up tie the strings tightly around your shoes.*

6. *As you walk around on your tin can stilts, think about how God is the one who is really in control of everything (including how tall you are). Thank Him for taking care of you and helping you not to worry.*

☐ *Draw a star in this box when you've read Matthew 6:27, 31-34.*

Seek the Kingdom of God First

Jesus said that God gives us food, clothes, and everything else that we need. He promised that if you "seek first his kingdom and his righteousness, all these things will be given to you as well." That means that God wants you to think most about how you can live for Him. He will take care of all your other needs.

Who rules you? If Jesus is your king, draw a crown on His head.

Find the Hidden Symbols for God's Kingdom

The kingdom of heaven is made up of the people who want to follow Jesus and make Him their king. Jesus wants you to be a part of the kingdom by letting Him lead you. He wants you to help others come into His kingdom.

Jesus compared the kingdom to many things. The Bible verses listed below tell us what some of those symbols are. *Look up the verses and write the words in the blanks. When you have filled in all the blanks, find the symbols that are hidden in the crown and circle them.*

The kingdom of heaven is like _ _ _ _ _ _ _ _ hidden in a field.
Matthew 13:44

The kingdom of heaven is like a business-man who found a _ _ _ _ _ of great price and sold all he had to buy it.
Matthew 13:45, 46

The kingdom of heaven is a like a _ _ _ that was let down into the lake and caught all kinds of fish.
Matthew 13:47, 48

The kingdom of heaven is like a _ _ _ _ who forgave a man who owed him money.
Matthew 18:23-35

Draw a star in this box when you've read Matthew 6:33; 13:44-48; and 18:23-35.

As We Forgive

In the Lord's Prayer, Jesus said "Forgive us our debts, as we also have forgiven our debtors." Jesus was saying that we need to ask for forgiveness of our sins, and we need to forgive people who sin against us. Jesus said that if you forgive others, God will forgive you, but if you don't forgive others, God won't forgive you.

If you don't forgive someone, that is called "holding a grudge." Holding a grudge in your heart can keep you from feeling close to God and can keep Him from forgiving you.

Draw a Grudge Monster

If a grudge were a monster, what do you think it would look like?
Ugly! Draw an ugly grudge in this heart.

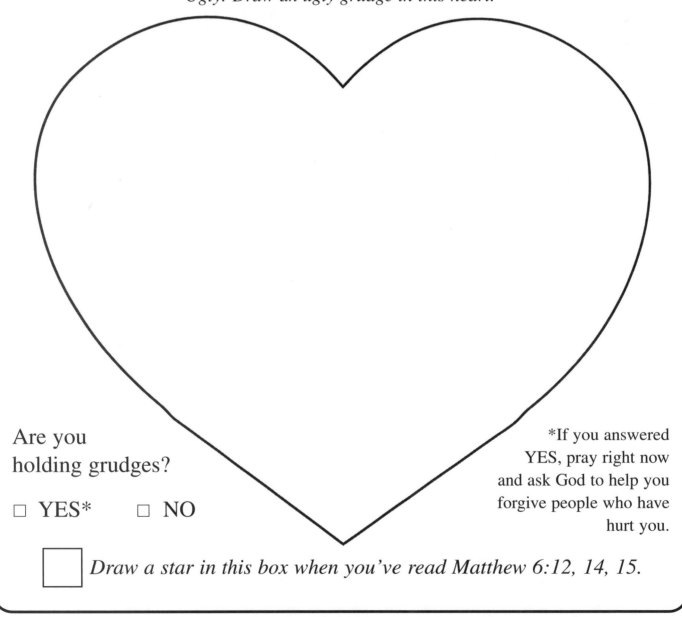

Are you
holding grudges?

□ YES*   □ NO

*If you answered
YES, pray right now
and ask God to help you
forgive people who have
hurt you.

☐ *Draw a star in this box when you've read Matthew 6:12, 14, 15.*

Pray for Your Enemies

Jesus says, "You have heard that it was said, 'Love your neighbor and hate your enemy.' But I tell you: Love your enemies and pray for those who persecute you." Jesus wants us to love everyone, even people who are mean to us.

What can you pray when your pray for your enemies? You can pray that you'll understand why they have acted that way. You can ask that they'll stop being mean to you, and that the Lord will soften your heart so you can forgive them. Can you think of something else that you can pray for them?

Forgiveness Autograph Book

Make an autograph book for your friends to sign. You can pray for people you wouldn't want to sign your autograph book then when you have forgiven them, ask them to sign it. You can look at your autographs later and be reminded of God's forgiveness!

What You Need

- ten sheets of typing paper
- scissors
- stapler
- different colored pens or markers

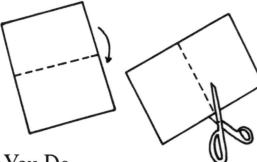

What You Do

1. Fold ten sheets of typing paper in half as shown.

2. Cut along the fold.

3. Fold the half sheets as shown.

4. Staple along the fold.

5. Decorate the cover by writing AUTOGRAPHS all over it in different colors of ink.

☐ *Draw a star in this box when you've read Matthew 5:43, 44.*

Deliver Us from Evil

When you're tempted to do something wrong, PRAY! God can give you the strength to resist, and He can help you know how to get out of a situation. Praying ahead of time can also help you know what to do. *Write what God wants you to do when you're in situations like these, then find the hidden letters P, R, A, and Y in each picture.*

Your best friend didn't have time to study for today's test. She wants to copy from your paper.

God would want me to

_____

_____

_____

You're at a friend's house and he turns on a dirty movie.

God would want me to

_____

_____

_____

The ice cream man is on your street. You don't have enough money to buy anything. Your brother has money in his bank, but he isn't home.

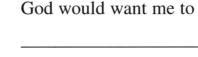

God would want me to

_____

_____

_____

Your friends are making fun of a new kid at school.

God would want me to

_____

_____

_____

☐ *Draw a star in this box when you've read Matthew 6:13.*

In Jesus' Name

Jesus said, "You may ask me for anything in my name, and I will do it." He also said, "I tell you the truth, my Father will give you whatever you ask in my name." We need to be sure what we are praying for is what God wants and that it isn't something selfish or wrong.

Jesus told us to pray "in His name." When a police officer says, "Stop in the name of the law!" he is saying the law has given him the right to tell someone to stop. When we pray "in the name of Jesus," we are saying Jesus has given us the right to come before God.

Make a Stamp of Jesus' Name

What You Need

- twine
- scissors
- glue
- small box or block of wood
- paint
- paper plate

What You Do

1. *Cut the twine to form Jesus' name backward as shown.*

2. *Glue the pieces of twine onto the box or wood block to make a stamp. Let dry.*

3. *Pour paint onto the paper plate and dip the stamp into it. Press the stamp to fill in the blank at the bottom of this page. You can also use it to make stationery.*

We Pray in the Name of _____

Stamp of Jesus Here

Draw a star in this box when you've read John 14:14; 16:23; Hebrews 10:19, 20; James 4:3; and I John 5:14, 15.

Humble Prayer

Jesus wants us to remember that we're talking to God when we pray. He said that when we pray, it's good to go to a quiet room where no one else will see or hear us. If we do that, we can talk to God and tell Him what's in our hearts without trying to impress other people with lots of fancy words.

When we pray, we need to praise God, not ourselves. Jesus wants us to ask God for forgiveness for what we do wrong, not pump ourselves up by praying about how great we are and how bad others are. He told this story to help people understand.

The Pharisee and the Tax Collector

To decode the story that Jesus told, change every A to O, every O to A, every E to I, every I to E, and every Z to U.

Twa min wint ta thi timpli ta proy. Ani wos o chzrch liodir collid o Phoresii. Thi athir wos o tox callictar. Thi Phoresii staad ond proyid, "Gad, Thonk yaz thot E'm nat bod leki athir piapli ond thot tox callictar. E da lats af gaad thengs."

Bzt thi tox callictar wazldn't ivin laak zp taword hiovin. Hi het hes awn chist ond soed, "Gad, fargevi mi. E'm o sennir."

Jiszs soed thi tox callictar wint hami reght weth Gad, bzt nat thi Phoresii. Jiszs soed thot whaivir lefts hemsilf zp well bi pzt dawn ond whaivir es hzmbli well bi leftid zp ta levi weth Gad.

Make a pipe cleaner Pharisee and tax collector to act out the story.

What You Need

• 3 pipe cleaners

• wire cutters

What You Do

1. *Bend a pipe cleaner in half.*
2. *Bend out the ends for feet. Bend the top into a circle that will be the head.*
3. *Cut a pipe cleaner in half.*
4. *Twist one half of the pipe cleaner around the neck area to form arms.*
5. *Repeat for the other puppet.*
6. *Use your puppets to act out the story.*

☐ *Draw a star in this box when you've read Matthew 6:5-7 and Luke 18:9-14.*

Repent

Jesus told people to repent. To repent means to turn away from sin. When you do wrong things God is ready and waiting to forgive you if you ask Him. Jesus said that "there is rejoicing in the presence of the angels of God over one sinner who repents." God loves you and wants you to come to Him when you've done something wrong.

Jesus told this story about a run-away son to show how lovingly God forgives His children and welcomes them back to Him when they repent.

The Prodigal Son

A 🧔 had 2 ☀️s. The younger ☀️ asked the 🧔 2 give him $. The 🧔 gave each ☀️ 1/2 of his $. The younger ☀️ took 🪙 -B of his $ & went F + ⭐ -ST A+ 〰️ -VES & wasted it 📱 wild living.

After the ☀️ had S+ 🖊️ +T 🪙 -B the $, he was very hungry. 1 day while he was feeding someone's 🐖, he got so hungry T+ 🎩 he 🪵 have eaten the 🐖 food, 🔘 -ON no 1 🪵 give him any.

T+ 🐔 the ☀️ came 2 his senses & thought about H+ 🐄 -C his 🧔 's workers had more than enough 2 eat & H+ 🐄 -C he was starving. He

Repent (continued)

decided 2 [stoplight] 2 his [house] & 2 [bee] + come 1 of his workers.

While the [sun] was F+ [star] -ST N the distance, the [man] [saw] him & felt great [heart] 4 him. The [man] ran 2 his [sun], [hug], & [kiss].

The [sun] said, "Father, [eye] have sinned against heaven & against U. [eye] no longer deserve 2 [bee] called your [sun]."

[button] -ON [man] told his workers 2 put the best [robe] [on] his [sun], a [ring] [on] his [hand], & [sandals] [on] his [feet]. The [man] told them 2 F + 6 -S a [table] 2 celebrate. He said, "4 this [sun] of mine was [grave] & is alive again; he was lost and is found." So they [bee] +gan 2 celebrate.

[ ] *Draw a star in this box when you've read Mark 1:15; Luke 15:10-24; and I John 1:9.*

Ask, Seek, Knock

Jesus said, "Ask and it will be given to you; seek and you will find; knock and the door will be opened to you. For everyone who asks receives; he who seeks finds; and to him who knocks, the door will be opened."

God will always answer your prayers. Sometimes you ask and you might have to wait for an answer, and when you look, the answer may not always be what you expect, but it will be what's best for you. When we knock on God's door, He will always answer.

Make a door hanger to remind others to knock before entering and to remind yourself that when you pray, nothing will come between you and God.

What You Need

- a copy of the door hanger on thin cardboard
- scissors
- crayons or markers
- decorations
- glue

What You Do

1. Make a photocopy of this page or tear it out of this book (after you have read page 24).

2. Color the door hanger with crayons or markers.

3. Glue it to thin cardboard.

4. Cut out the door hanger.

5. Glue on scraps of ribbons, sequins, or other decorations.

6. When it is dry, hang it on your bedroom doorknob.

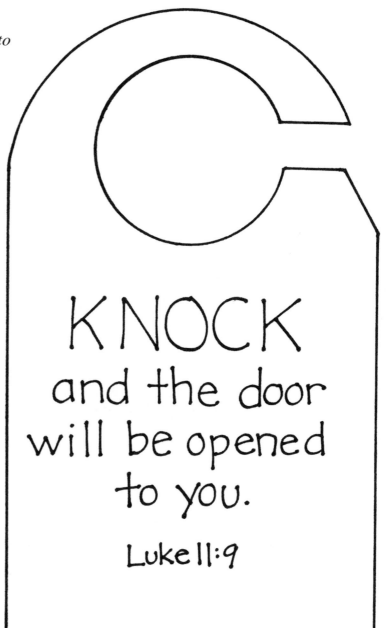

KNOCK
and the door
will be opened
to you.

Luke 11:9

Draw a star in this box when you've read Luke 11:9, 10.

The Friend at Midnight

Draw lines between the words in this story. The first line has been done to get you started.

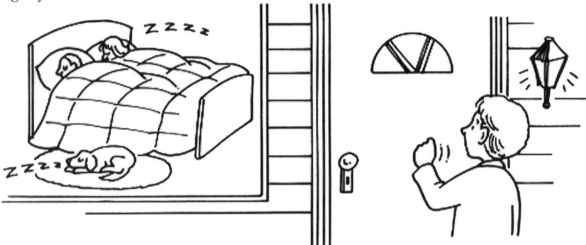

Jesus|said|"Suppose|you|went|to|a|friend|at|midnight andsaid, 'Pleaselendmethreeloavesofbread.Another friendofmineisvisitingandIdon'thaveanythingtofeed him.'

"Yourfriendanswersfrominsidehishouse, 'Don't botherme.I'veshutthedoorandmychildrenareinbed withme.Ican'tgetupandgiveyoubread.'Eventhoughthe manwon'tgiveyouthefoodbecauseyou'rehisfriend, hewillgetupandgiveyouallyouneedbecauseyoukeep knockinganddon'tgiveup."

JesuswasteachingthatifyouaskGodforsomethingand don'tquitwaitingforit,Hewillalwaysansweryou.Whatif thepersonneedingbreadonlyknockedoncelightly,left,and forgotaboutaskingforthebread?Hegotthebreadbecausehe believedhisfriendwouldgiveittohimandhedidn'tquit waitinguntilhegotit.Sometimeswehavetowaitforan answer,buttrustingGodtoansweryourprayersispartofwhat itmeanstohavefaith.

☐ *Draw a star in this box when you've read Luke 11:5-8.*

Torn Paper Picture

Are you waiting for an answer to a prayer? Tear pieces of colored paper and glue them onto this page to make a picture of a blessing that is coming to you.

The Unfair Judge and the Fair Judge

Jesus told this story to encourage His followers to keep praying and not give up.
Fill in the missing vowels (A, E, I, O, and U).

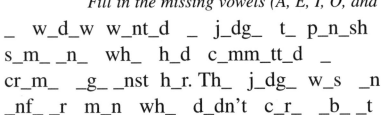

_ w_d_w w_nt_d _ j_dg_ t_ p_n_sh
s_m__n_ wh_ h_d c_mm_tt_d _
cr_m_ _g_ _nst h_r. Th_ j_dg_ w_s _n
_nf__r m_n wh_ d_dn't c_r_ _b__t
G_d _r p__pl_. _t f_rst h_ w__ldn't h_lp th_ w_d_w, b_t th_n
h_ th__ght, "_'ll p_n_sh th_ cr_m_n_l b_c__s_ _f _ d_n't, th_
w_d_w w_ll k__p c_m_ng b_ck _nd w_ll w__r m_ __t."

 _f _n _nf__r j_dg_ w__ld h_lp th_t w_d_w, w__ldn't _
f__r j_dg_?

 G_d _s _ v_ry f__r j_dg_. J_s_s s__d th_t G_d w_ll
_lw_ys _nsw_r __r pr_y_rs.

If a bad judge would help her, wouldn't a good judge?
Make this boomerang and decide to keep coming back to God for answers to your prayers.

What You Need

• 2 tongue depressors (from a doctor's office, a pharmacy, or a medical supply store)
• 2 small rubber bands
• pen

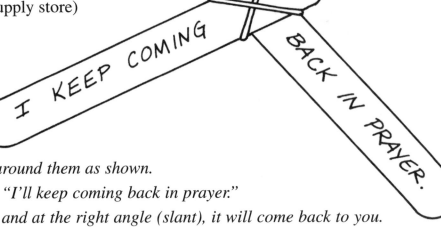

What You Do

1. *Cross the depressors at one end.*
2. *Stretch the rubber bands around them as shown.*
3. *Write on your boomerang "I'll keep coming back in prayer."*
4. *If you throw it far enough and at the right angle (slant), it will come back to you.*

Draw a star in this box when you've read Luke 18:1-8.

The Mystery Word

If you cross out the foods in the lists below, you will be left with some clues about the mystery word. *After you have solved the mystery, look up the Bible verses to make sure that you were right.*

Clue #1

POPCORN SPAGHETTI JESUS OAT-MEAL APPLESAUCE AND CARROTS OKRA MANY SALAD OTHER LASAGNA BIBLE TAFFY PEOPLE GRAPES MILK DID BOLOGNA BREAD THIS.

Clue #2

CEREAL THE BREAD DISCIPLES NOODLES DID CORNDOGS NOT HAM JELLY PICKLES DO SPINACH THIS WHILE TOMATOES PEACHES JESUS WAS TACOS WITH POPSICLES THEM, BANANAS COOKIES BUT CRACKERS CHEESE HE SAID THEY BEETS WOULD RADISHES DO IT WHEN HE PUDDING WAS POTATOES GONE.

Mystery Word

__ __ __ __ __ __ __ __ __ __

Clue #3

DONUTS JESUS WATERMELON SAID TO BROCCOLI DO IT PANCAKES SE-CRETLY AND SANDWICHES GOD CHILI WILL ORANGES BLESS BEANS YOU HAMBURGERS.

Clue #4

BAGELS PEOPLE DOING PEAS EGGPLANT THIS DO NOT EAT MARSHMALLOWS DURING FUDGE A BACON TIME OF GELATIN EXTRA YOGURT PRAYER TO RAISINS PIE GET STRAWBERRIES CLOSER PIZZA TO GOD.

Last chance clue.

If you can't figure out the mystery word from the other clues, write the first letter of each of these foods.

☐ *Draw a star in this box when you've read Matthew 6:16-18; and 9:14, 15.*

Two Agree in Prayer

Jesus said that if two people agree about anything they pray for, God will answer them. Jesus also said that where two or three Christians get together, He is with them.

A big part of being a Christian is helping other people, and a great way to do that is through prayer. *Ask someone you trust to be your prayer pal. Each day you can pray for each other. To let each other know what prayers you need, you can trade private notes that are written in invisible ink. Here are some recipes.*

Salt Water Invisible Ink

Mix 1 teaspoon salt and 1 teaspoon hot water to make the ink. Dip a toothpick or paintbrush in the ink and write your message lightly on a piece of paper. Let the message dry for at least half an hour, then give it to your prayer pal. He can make the message reappear by rubbing it with a pencil.

Plain Water Invisible Writing

Wet a sheet of paper and pat it with a sponge. (Make sure it's not dripping!) Lay the damp paper on a flat surface and cover it with a dry sheet of paper. Write a message on the dry paper with a dull pencil. Press firmly so the message makes a dent in the damp paper underneath. Throw away the dry paper. The message on the damp paper will disappear when it dries. Give it to your prayer pal. She can make the message reappear by wetting the paper again.

> Please pray for me to love my sister more.

Milk Ink

Lightly write a message on a 4 x 5 file card with a toothpick or paintbrush dipped in whole milk. Let it dry and give it to your prayer pal. She can make the message appear by using a plastic knife to scratch lead off the point of a pencil onto the paper and then rubbing the lead over the message with her finger.

Draw a star in this box when you've read Matthew 18:19, 20.

Faith to Move a Mountain

One morning Jesus was hungry and hoped to find fruit on a fig tree. When He saw that it didn't have any figs on it, He said, "May you never bear fruit again!" and the tree died. When His disciples saw what happened, they were amazed at His power. Jesus told them, "Have faith in God. I tell you the truth, if anyone says to this mountain, 'Go, throw yourself into the sea,' and does not doubt in his heart but believes that what he says will happen, it will be done for him. Therefore I tell you, whatever you ask for in prayer, believe that you have received it, and it will be yours."

Jesus said that if we really believe our prayers will be answered; we will receive whatever we ask. We need to be sure what we pray for is what God wants and that it isn't selfish or wrong.

Play Faithball

Use your faith to knock problems into the sea.

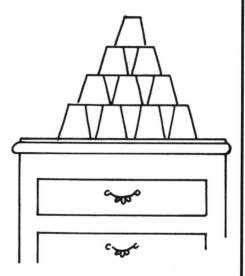

What You Need

- 1 or more players
- 10 paper cups for each player
- permanent marker for each player
- tennis ball (outdoors), or Nerf ball (indoors), or Styrofoam ball (indoors)

What You Do

1. *On the inside of the cups, write some problems you're trusting God to help you solve. Stack the cups in a mountain shape on a table.*
2. *If you have permission to write on the ball, write FAITH on it. If you can't write on the ball, just think of it as your faith.*
3. *To play alone: Stand back and throw the ball. Is your faith strong enough to knock the whole mountain of problems into the sea below? Keep trying!*
4. *To play with 2 or more: Take turns trying to knock down your own mountain. If someone is having a hard time knocking his or hers down, encourage and cheer that person. See what a difference encouraging each other can make?*
5. *Another way to play with 2 or more: Try to knock down someone else's mountain of problems. How does it feel to help someone else get rid of a problem? How does it feel to have someone help you get rid of yours? Feels pretty good, doesn't it?*

Draw a star in this box when you've read Matthew 21:18-22 and Mark 11:12-14, 20-24.

Faith the Size of a Mustard Seed

One day Jesus said to His disciples, "If you have faith as small as a mustard seed, you can say to this mountain, 'Move from here to there' and it will move. Nothing will be impossible for you." Jesus was saying that if we trust God even a tiny bit, He will help us do things that even seem impossible.

How Big Is a Mustard Seed?

Mustard seeds are very tiny. The one in the circle is the size they really are! There are three others hidden on this page. Can you find them? Good luck!

Ask your mom if she has any real mustard seeds in the kitchen for you to see. If she doesn't have any, you can find mustard seeds in the spice aisle of some supermarkets.

Draw or glue mustard seeds on these letters

FAITH MOVES MOUNTAINS

Make a Colored Sugar Mountain

Make this mountain to remind yourself that mustard seed sized faith can move mountains.

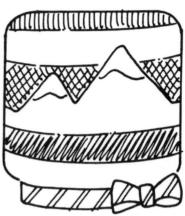

What You Need

- a baby food jar
- 1 cup sugar
- 5 paper cups
- red, yellow, and blue food coloring
- spoon
- toothpick
- scrap piece of ribbon (optional)
- glue

What You Do

1. Divide the sugar into five paper cups.
2. Put a drop of red food coloring into one cup to make pink sugar, a drop of yellow into the second cup, and a drop of blue into the third cup. Stir. Make lavender sugar in the fourth cup by pouring in half of the pink sugar and a little of the blue sugar. Stir. Leave one cup of sugar white.
3. Make a sunset sky by pouring thin layers of pink, yellow, and blue sugar into the baby food jar until it is about 3/4 full.
4. Use the handle of the spoon to push sugar away from the side of the jar, leaving a triangle-shaped empty space.
5. Pour a little white sugar into the space to look like snow on the top of the mountain.
6. Fill the rest of the space with lavender sugar to look like a mountain.
7. Continue to layer sugars until the jar is full.
8. Put glue around the rim of the jar and screw on the lid. Wipe off any extra glue.
9. Turn the jar upside-down.
10. If you want to decorate the lid, glue a scrap of ribbon around the sides of it.

Draw a star in this box when you've read Matthew 17:20.

Believe

To have faith that God will answer your prayers means you believe that He will help you. If you have faith, God will answer your prayers.

Decode what Jesus said about having faith.

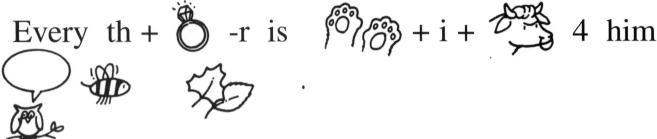

Believe and Pray

Find the triangle above each blank in the code. Then fill the correct letter in the blank to find what Matthew 21:22 says about believing.

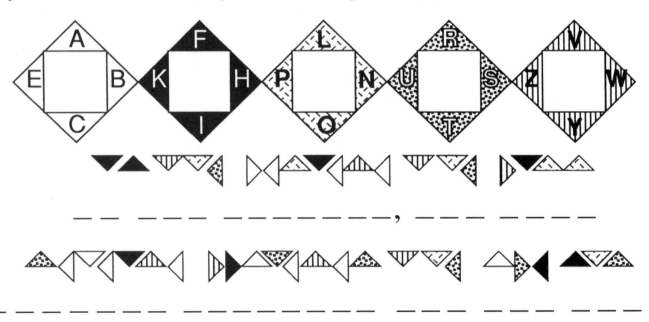

Draw a star in this box when you've read Matthew 21:22 and Mark 9:23.

My Yoke Is Easy

Some people try to get to heaven by doing good works, but no one can do anything good enough to deserve living with God forever. Trying to get to heaven that way only makes people tired, burdened, and discouraged; it doesn't get them anywhere. Jesus wants us to trust Him, not ourselves, as the only way to heaven. When we do that, our load is light; we obey and do good works for the right reason–because we love God.

A yoke is a wooden bar that fits two or more animals so they can pull a load together that would be too heavy for one to pull alone. Jesus wants us to wear His yoke. To wear His yoke means that we trust Him to save us and help us. With His help, our load is much lighter.

Unscramble the BOLD, CAPITALIZED words to find out what Jesus said. Then look up Matthew 11:28-30 to see if your answers are right.

"Come to me, all you who are weary and **RDENBUDE** _____, and I will give you **STER** _____. Take my **KYOE** _____ upon you and **REANL** _____ from me, for I am gentle and humble in **REHAT** _____, and you will find **STER** _____for your souls. For my **KYOE** _____is easy and my burden is **GIHTL**_____."

Would you like to be sure you will go to heaven?

You can if you put your trust in Jesus as your Savior (the one who saves you) and promise to follow Him as your Lord (the one who rules you). If you believe the things in this prayer, pray them in your own words and you can be sure you will go to heaven because of your faith in Jesus (Romans 10:8-10).

Dear God, please forgive me for what I have done wrong. I believe that You will forgive my sins because Your son Jesus died for me and You raised Him from the dead. Thank You for saving me. Please keep my faith strong and help me do what You want me to do. In Jesus name I pray. Amen.

☐ *Draw a star in this box when you've read Matthew 11:28-30; John 3:16; 14:6; Romans 3:20; 10:8-10; 11:6; Galatians 2:16.*

Lighten Someone's Burden with a Balloon

Jesus said His yoke is easy and His burden is light. You can lighten someone's burden by telling that person about Jesus. A fun way to send the good news is by helium balloon.

What You Need

- helium balloon on a string
- message on this page
- scissors
- pen
- fluorescent markers, if you have them
- self-adhesive paper
- hole punch

What You Do

1. *Cut out the message below (information about how to accept Jesus is on the other side of it).*
2. *Fill in the blanks. Make a bright border around both sides of the message with fluorescent markers if you have them and seal the message between two pieces of self-adhesive paper.*
3. *Punch a hole in the message and tie it to a helium balloon.*
4. *Let it go up into the sky. Pray that the person who finds the message will receive Jesus as Lord and Savior.*

I sent this message to you by helium balloon!
Please write to let me know you received it.

My name is _____

My church

address is _____

_____

_____

Photo Reminders

Make these stand-up, picture cutouts to remind yourself to pray for other people.

What You Need

- photos and permission to use them
- scissors
- pen
- clean Styrofoam plate or meat tray
- glue
- clean Styrofoam cup or fast food box lid

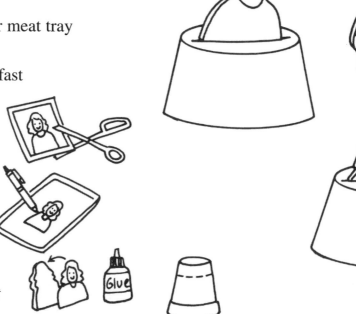

What You Do

1. *Find or take pictures of people you want to remember in your prayers. Be sure to get permission to cut up the pictures. (You don't want to use instant photos because they split apart when cut.)*

2. *Carefully cut around the head and body of the person in each picture.*

3. *Lay the cut-out on a Styrofoam plate and trace around it with a pen.*

4. *Cut out the Styrofoam outline and glue it to the back of your picture. (Be careful not to get any glue on the front of the picture.)*

5. *When it's dry, cut away any Styrofoam that shows from behind your friend.*

6. *To make a stand, cut around a cup, about one inch from the bottom as shown. Turn the cup upside-down and make a slit. If you're using a Styrofoam fast food box instead, cut off the lid of the box and make a slit in it.*

7. *Insert the picture into the slit of the stand.*

8. *Put your picture friends in a spot where you'll see them as you are about to pray.*

These pictures can remind you to include your friends in your prayers.

Silent Prayers

The Bible says we ought to pray all the time. That doesn't mean that you have to be on your knees day and night, though! What it means is that God wants you to be silently talking and listening to Him throughout the day. *Unscramble the simple prayers below that you could say in each of these everyday situations.*

1. YOU HAVE 20 MINUTES TO COMPLETE THE TEST.

   lePaes pleh em rebmemre hawt I dutsdie.

   _____

2. sePlea formcot ym tersis dna pelh em wonk tawh I nca od orf reh.

   _____

   _____

3. leaPse elph ym therbro nda steris ot teg nalog retteb.

   _____

   _____

4. Pealse ahle eht repnos ni ahtt lubamane.

   _____

5. seaPle hlep em keam a denfir uto fo sith yug.

   _____

   _____

6. knahT uoy rof kmanig hucs a abetuiflu rolwd!

   _____

   _____

☐ *Draw a star in this box when you've read Luke 18:1.*

God Gives Good Gifts

Imagine that you're a parent and ask yourself these questions Jesus asked in Matthew 7:9-11 and Luke 11:11-13.

If your child asked for this, would you give him this? No.

If your child asked for this, would you give him this? No.

If your child asked for this, would you give him this? No.

Of course you wouldn't give your child something that is bad for him. Jesus said that if people who sin know how to give good gifts, then God, who is perfect, knows how to give great gifts. One of the gifts He promised to give us is the Holy Spirit.

You and a friend can act out these questions that Jesus asked. You can make props out of craft dough.

Craft Dough

(Don't make half of the recipe or double it. It won't work.)

What You Need

- 1 cup salt
- 4 cups pre-sifted all-purpose flour
- about 1 1/2 cups water
- paper plate
- paint
- paintbrushes
- cupcake wrappers
- clear acrylic spray

What You Do

1. *Stir salt and flour together.*
2. *Add water a little at a time until the mixture is a dough you can handle. (You may not need all of the water.)*
3. *Squeeze the dough for two or three minutes until it isn't grainy anymore.*
4. *Shape the dough into bread, a stone, a fish, a snake, an egg, a scorpion, and a dove (the symbol for the Holy Spirit).*
5. *Lay your shapes on a paper plate and prick them all over with a toothpick.*
6. *Dry them for 1-3 minutes in the microwave (large pieces take a little longer) or let them air dry for at least 48 hours.*
7. *Paint the shapes with water colors or acrylic paints.*

☐ *Draw a star in this box when you've read Matthew 7:9-11 and Luke 11:11-13*

Jesus' Sheep Know His Voice

Jesus said "I am the good shepherd; I know my sheep and my sheep know me."

If you are one of Jesus' sheep, write your name on the lamb He is holding.

Become One of His Sheep

You can become one of Jesus' sheep by asking Him to be your Savior (the one who gets rid of your sin so you are able to go to heaven) and Lord (the one you follow). If you want Jesus to be your Lord and Savior, pray a prayer like this one in your own words.

Dear God,

Thank you for sending Jesus. I want Him to be my Savior and my Lord. Please forgive me for my sins and help me follow Him all of my life like a sheep follows its shepherd.

In Jesus' name I pray. Amen

Draw a star in this box when you've read John 10:14, 15.

Know His Voice

Jesus said that His sheep listen to Him and know His voice. When you pray, you get to know Jesus and how He answers prayer. Here is a fun game that will help you remember to listen for Jesus' answers to your prayers.

The Shepherd's Voice Game

One player is a sheep and wears a blindfold; another is the good shepherd. The other players all speak to the sheep at once. The player who is the good shepherd speaks in his or her natural voice. The others try to drown out the good shepherd's voice and trick the sheep by disguising their voices.

The sheep points toward the voice he thinks is the good shepherd's. If right, the sheep gets two points and none if wrong. Then the sheep tries to point and guess who the other voices are. Once the sheep points at a player and guesses, correctly or not, that player is silent. The sheep gets a point for each player he or she can name correctly. Players take turns being the sheep. The player with the most points wins.

☐ *Draw a star in this box when you've read John 10:4, 27, 28.*

Help from the Holy Spirit

Jesus told those who believed in Him that after He went to heaven God would send the Holy Spirit to teach all things, to remind believers of everything Jesus said, to guide us into all truth, and to tell them what is yet to come. After Jesus went to heaven, the Holy Spirit did come.

When you pray, listen for the Holy Spirit. He is called the Counselor because He tells us what God wants us to know and do. He is called the Comforter because He gives us peace when we're upset.

Jesus compared the Holy Spirit to the wind. He said, "The wind blows wherever it pleases. You hear its sound, but you cannot tell where it comes from or where it is going. So it is with everyone born of the Spirit. God speaks to us through the Holy Spirit even though, just like the wind, we can't see Him.

Doves are a symbol of the Holy Spirit. *Make this dove wind chime to remind yourself that the Holy Spirit is as real as the wind.*

Dove Wind Chime

What You Need

- grown-up help
- 8 frozen juice lids
- nail, hammer
- thin paper
- twine or embroidery floss

- wire coat hanger
- cardboard or heavy paper
- tape
- pen
- scissors

- white spray paint
- old newspapers
- blue acrylic paint
- old toothbrush
- small piece of old screen

What You Do

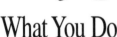
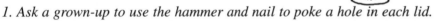

1. *Ask a grown-up to use the hammer and nail to poke a hole in each lid.*
2. *Put the lids on some old newspapers and spray paint them white. Let them dry.*
3. *Lay a piece of thin paper over this page and trace the dove onto it. Cut out the dove. Trace the paper dove onto cardboard or heavy paper and cut it out. Place a loop of tape under the cardboard dove and press it onto the center of a painted juice lid. Trace and cut out seven more cardboard doves to tape on the other juice lids.*
4. *Dip the toothbrush in the blue paint. Hold the screen over each lid and rub the toothbrush across it to make a speckled pattern on the lids.*
5. *Let everything dry and carefully take off the cardboard doves.*
6. *Ask a grown-up to bend the coat hanger in half and to bend the hook into a loop as shown.*
7. *Cut eight pieces of string, each about 18 inches long. Tie one end of each string to the hanger and the other end to a juice lid.*
8. *Hang your wind chime outside and let it remind you to listen for the Holy Spirit.*

☐ *Draw a star in this box when you've read John 3:8; 14:26; and 16:13.*

I Did It!

COMPLETED	DATE	COMPLETED	DATE
☐ Riddles about Jesus' Prayers	_____	☐ Ask, Seek, Knock	_____
☐ Prayer Pillowcase	_____	☐ The Friend at Midnight	_____
☐ The Lord's Prayer	_____	☐ Torn Paper Picture	_____
☐ Memorization Bath Stickers	_____	☐ The Unfair Judge and the Fair Judge	_____
☐ Hallowed Be Your Name	_____	☐ The Mystery Word	_____
☐ Your Will Be Done	_____	☐ Two Agree in Prayer	_____
☐ Our Daily Bread	_____	☐ Faith to Move a Mountain	_____
☐ God Will Feed You	_____	☐ Faith the Size of a Mustard Seed	_____
☐ God Will Clothe You	_____	☐ Make a Colored Sugar Mountain	_____
☐ Don't Worry	_____	☐ Believe	_____
☐ Seek the Kingdom of God First	_____	☐ My Yoke Is Easy	_____
☐ As We Forgive	_____	☐ Lighten Someone's Burden	_____
☐ Pray for Your Enemies	_____	☐ Photo Reminders	_____
☐ Deliver Us from Evil	_____	☐ Silent Prayers	_____
☐ In Jesus' Name	_____	☐ God Gives Good Gifts	_____
☐ Humble Prayer	_____	☐ Jesus' Sheep Know His Voice	_____
☐ Repent	_____	☐ Help from the Holy Spirit	_____

Answers

Page 8
1. Yes; 2. No; 3. No; 4. Yes;
5. Yes; 6. No; 7. Yes

Page 9
1-D
2-A
3-E
4-F
5-C
6-B

Page 10

One day Jesus, His disciples (followers), and his **mother** (Mary) attended a **wedding**. After a while, the host ran out of **wine**, and Mary told Jesus. Jesus **asked** what Mary wanted Him to do. Mary didn't **answer** but she told the servants to do whatever Jesus told **them** to do.

There were six **stone** water pots there, which could hold **twenty** or thirty gallons each. Jesus said to **fill** the pots with **water**, and the servants did. Jesus then told one of the servants to give **some** to the host of the wedding **feast**.

The wedding host didn't believe the wine he tasted had once been water. He said he was happily surprised that the groom had **saved** the best wine for last.

Jesus did this first **miracle** in Cana of Galilee and His disciples believed that He was God's Son.

Page 13

One day **Jesus** told **Simon Peter** to take his **boat** into deep **water** and let **down** his **net** to **catch** a lot of **fish**. **Simon Peter** said, "We **fished** all **night** and didn't **catch** anything, but I'll let **down** the **net** again anyway." After he **dropped** it, the **net** filled up with so many **fish** that it **broke**. The **fish** filled two **ships** and the boats began to **sink**.

Simon Peter and everyone else were **amazed**. Simon Peter **fell** at Jesus' **knees**. Jesus said, "From now on, you will **catch** men." He meant that Simon Peter and his fishing **partners** would **bring people** into the **kingdom** of **God.**

Page 20

Answers—Jesus' Ministry

Answers

Page 22

Page 23

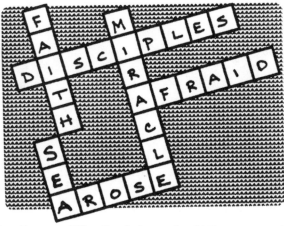

Page 26

One evening after Jesus taught a crowd in the **desert**, His disciples asked Him to send the people away so they could buy themselves food in the village. Jesus said, "They don't need to **leave**. You give them something to eat." Andrew said, "There's a young **boy** here with five loaves of bread and two small **fish**, but that is not enough to feed this crowd of people." Jesus said, "Bring the boy to me." Jesus also asked the people to sit on the grass in **groups** of fifties and hundreds.

Then Jesus held the five loaves and two fish, looked up to **heaven**, and gave thanks. He gave the bread and fish to the disciples, and they passed out the food to the people. More than 5,000 people were fed that day. Afterward, the disciples picked up **twelve** baskets of leftovers.

Another time, Jesus had been teaching more than 4,000 people for three days in the wilderness. Now Jesus knew that they were hungry and didn't want to send them away without eating because they might **faint**. The disciples only had seven **loaves** of bread and a few fish. Jesus gave **thanks**, divided the bread and fish, and gave them to the disciples, who in turn gave the food to the people. Once again, everyone in the crowd was fed, and this time there were seven baskets of leftovers.

Pages 30-31 1-C; 2-F; 3-A; 4-E; 5-D; 6-B

Page 39

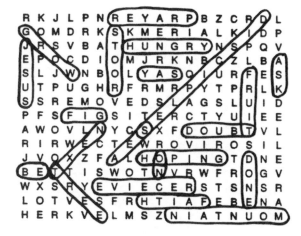

Answers

Page 50

Page 69
Luke 13:10-17

Page 77
Mark 10:46-52

Page 63
Matthew 12:9-13

Page 62
Mark 7:31-37
(2 different body parts)

Page 83
John 18:10, 11

Page 51

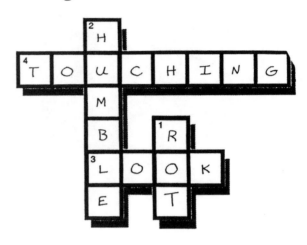

Page 54

When Jesus came to the **gate** of the city of Nain, He saw a **dead** man being carried out. This man was the only son of a **widow** (a woman whose husband had died). When Jesus saw the mother of the dead man, He had compassion (great love) for her and said, "Don't cry." Then He **touched** the coffin. The **people** carrying the coffin stopped. Jesus said, "Young man, I say to you, arise."

Suddenly the dead man sat up and began to **speak**. The people were **amazed** and praised God saying, "A great prophet is among us" and "God has **visited** His people." Throughout Judea and the other regions **around** it, the word **went** out about **Jesus.**

Page 57

Arm on bed,
food on table,
position of shoes,
another man next to bed,
girl's eyes open,
foot sticking out,
smile

Page 60

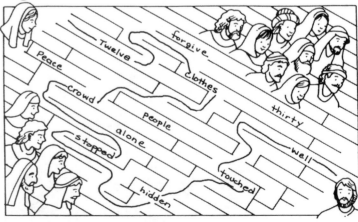

Answers—Jesus' Ministry

Answers

Page 61   Do you believe I am able to do this?

Page 67

(The people thought an angle would stir the water at the pool of Bethesda.)	~~The sick man's mat was too heavy for him to carry.~~	(The healed man blamed the person who healed him for causing him to break the sabbath.)
(The people thought the first one to step into the pool after an angel stirred the waters would be healed.)	(It was against the law to carry a mat on the sabbath.)	When the healed man learned Jesus' name, he kept it a secret to protect Jesus.
~~The man Jesus healed had been sick for 52 years.~~	(The healed man told the Jewish leaders he didn't know who made him well.)	(The Jewish leaders wanted to kill Jesus for healing on the sabbath.)

Page 68   1. Jesus; 2. disturbed; 3. foams; 4. faith; 5. believe; 6. dead; 7. stood; 8. alone; 9. prayer

Page 70   Doing what God wants always pleases Him.

Page 72   Say thanks to God.

Page 73   1. Jesus; 2. Family and friends; 3. Food; 4. Home; 5. Love; 6. Holy Spirit; 7. Clothes; 8. Bible

Page 77   When **Jesus** and His disciples were **leaving** Jericho, a blind man named Bartimaeus sat begging by the **Highway.** When he heard that Jesus of Nazareth was passing by, he **began** to cry out, "Jesus, Son of David, have **mercy** on me."

   Jesus **stopped** walking and told some of the people to bring Bartimaeus to Him. They said to the **blind** man, "Take **comfort.** Stand up; He's calling for you." And he **stood** and went to Jesus.

   Jesus said, "What do you want me to do to you?" The blind man said, "I want to **receive** my sight."

   Jesus said, "Go your way; your **faith** has made you whole." Right away Bartimaeus received his **sight** and followed Jesus, glorifying God. And when all the people saw it, they gave **praise** to God.

Page 84   1. daughter; 2. son; 3. Lazarus; 4. servant; 5. centurion; 6. ten lepers

Answers

Page 89 1. day; 2. mountain; 3. Peter; 4. thanks; 5. hearing; 6. kids; 7. death; 8. will; 9. cross

Jesus took time to pray, and so should we.

Page 93 You shall not misuse the name of the Lord your God.

Page 99 treasure, pearl, net, king

Page 104 Two men went to the temple to pray. One was a church leader called a Pharisee. The other was a tax collector. The Pharisee stood and prayed, "God, Thank you that I'm not bad like other people and that tax collector. I do lots of good things."

But the tax collector wouldn't even look up toward heaven. He hit his own chest and said, "God forgive me. I'm a sinner."

Jesus said the tax collector went home right with God, but not the Pharisee. Jesus said that whoever lifts himself up will be put down and whoever is humble will be lifted up to live with God.

Page 108 Jesus said "Suppose you went to a friend at midnight and said, 'Please lend me three loaves of bread. Another friend of mine is visiting and I don't have anything to feed him.'

"Your friend answers from inside his house, 'Don't bother me. I've shut the door and my children are in bed with me. I can't get up and give you bread.' Even though the man won't give you the food because you're his friend, he will get up and give you all you need because you keep knocking and don't give up."

Jesus was teaching that if you ask God for something and don't quit waiting for it, He will always answer you. What if the person needing bread only knocked once lightly, left, and forgot about asking for the bread? He got the bread because he believed his friend would give it to him and he didn't quit waiting until he got it. Sometimes we have to wait for an answer, but trusting God to answer your prayers is part of what it means to have faith.

Answers

Page 110 A widow wanted a judge to punish someone who had committed a crime against her. The judge was an unfair man who didn't care about God or people. At first he wouldn't help the widow, but then he thought, "I'll punish the criminal because if I don't, the widow will keep coming back and will wear me out."
If an unfair judge would help that widow, wouldn't a fair judge?
God is a very fair judge. Jesus said that God will always answer our prayers.

Page 111 Clue #1 - Jesus and many other Bible people did this.
Clue #2 - The disciples did not do this while Jesus was with them, but He said they would do it when He was gone.
Clue #3 - Jesus said to do it secretly and God will bless you.
Clue #4 - People doing this do not eat during a time of prayer to get closer to God.

Mystery Word - Fasting

Page 114

Page 116 If you believe, you will receive whatever you ask for in prayer.

Page 117 "Come to me, all you who are weary and **burdened**, and I will give you **rest**. Take my **yoke** upon you and **learn** from me, for I am gentle and humble in **heart**, and you will find **rest** for your souls. For my **yoke** is easy and my burden is **light**."

Page 120 1. Please help me remember what I studied.
2. Please comfort my sister and help me know what I can do for her.
3. Please help my brother and sister to get along better.
4. Please heal the person in that ambulance.
5. Please help me make a friend out of this guy.
6. Thank you for making such a beautiful world!

Index

VOLUMES

Volume 1	Volume 2	Volume 3	Volume 4
Jesus' Early Years	**Jesus' Ministry**	**Following Jesus**	**The Love of Jesus**
Jesus Is Born	Jesus Works Miracles	Names of Jesus	Jesus Shows God's Love
Jesus Grows Up	Jesus Heals	Following Jesus	Jesus' Last Week
Jesus Prepares to Serve	Jesus Teaches Me to Pray	Learning to Love Like Jesus	Jesus Is Alive!

BIBLE STORY	LIFE AND LESSONS	BIBLE STORY	LIFE AND LESSONS
Healing of:		Jesus Is:	
10 Lepers	Vol. 2	the Light	Vol. 3
Blind Man	Vol. 3	the Redeemer	Vol. 3
Deaf and Mute Man	Vol. 3	the Resurrection and Life	Vol. 3
A Leper	Vol. 2	the Savior	Vol. 3
A Man's Hand	Vol. 2	the Son of God	Vol. 3
Blind Bartimaeus	Vol. 2	the Truth	Vol. 3
Centurion's Servant	Vol. 2	the Vine	Vol. 3
Epileptic Boy	Vol. 2	the Way	Vols. 3, 4
Malchus's Ear	Vol. 2	the Word	Vol. 3
Man Born Blind	Vol. 3	Jesus Loves Children	Vol. 4
Man with Dropsy	Vol. 2	Jesus Obeys Parents	Vol. 1
Official's Son	Vol. 2	Jesus Prayed	Vol. 2
Peter's Mother-in-Law	Vol. 2	Jesus Shows Compassion	Vol. 4
Paralytic	Vol. 2	Jesus Washes Disciples' Feet	Vols. 3, 4
Woman's Back	Vol. 2	Jesus' Family	Vol. 1
Woman Who Touched Hem	Vol. 2	Jesus' Genealogy	Vol. 1
Heaven	Vol. 4	Jesus' Trial Before Caiaphas	Vol. 4
How Much God Loves Us	Vol. 4	Jesus' Trial Before Pilate	Vol. 4
Humble Prayer	Vol. 2	John the Baptist	Vol. 1
I		Joseph's Dream	Vol. 1
I Am with You Always	Vol. 4	Judas Betrays Jesus	Vols. 1, 4
I Live/You Will Live	Vol. 4	Judge Not	Vol. 3
Include Others	Vol. 3	**K**	
J		Known by Fruits	Vol. 3
Jesus Clears the Temple	Vol. 4	**L**	
Jesus Died for Me	Vol. 4	Last Supper	Vol. 4
Jesus Eats with Sinners	Vol. 4	Lay Down Life for Friends	Vols. 3, 4
Jesus Has Overcome the World	Vol. 4	Lazarus and the Rich Man	Vol. 3
Jesus Is:		Life in New Testament Times	Vol. 1
'I AM'	Vol. 3	Light on a Hill	Vol. 3
Arrested	Vol. 4	Like Days of Noah	Vol. 4
Born	Vol. 1	Like Jonah's Three Days in Fish	Vol. 4
Buried	Vol. 4	Lord's Prayer	Vol. 2
Christ	Vols. 1, 3	Love Each Other	Vol. 4
Crucified and Dies	Vol. 4	Love Jesus Most	Vol. 4
God	Vol. 3	Love Me/Obey Me	Vol. 4
Immanuel	Vol. 3	Love One Another	Vol. 3
Tempted	Vol. 1	Loving Enemies	Vols. 2, 3
the Bread of Life	Vol. 3	**M**	
the Bridegroom	Vol. 3	Make Up Quickly	Vol. 3
the Chief Cornerstone	Vol. 3	Maps of New Testament Times	Vols. 1, 2
the Gate	Vol. 3	Mary and Martha	Vol. 3
the Gift of God	Vol. 3	Mary Anoints Jesus with Perfume	Vol. 4
the Good Shepherd	Vol. 3	Mary Visits Elizabeth	Vol. 1
the Lamb of God	Vol. 3		